Gold Diggers of 1933

Wisconsin/Warner Bros. Screenplay Series

Gold Diggers
of 1933

Edited with an introduction by

Arthur Hove

Published for the Wisconsin Center for Film and Theater Research by
The University of Wisconsin Press

Published 1980

The University of Wisconsin Press
114 North Murray Street
Madison, Wisconsin 53715

The University of Wisconsin Press, Ltd.
1 Gower Street
London WC1E 6 HA, England
First printing

Printed in the United States of America

For LC CIP information see the colophon

ISBN 0-299-08080-3 cloth; 0-299-08084-6 paper

Publication of this volume has been assisted by a grant from
The Brittingham Fund, Inc.

Contents

Foreword

In donating the Warner Film Library to the Wisconsin Center for Film and Theater Research in 1969, along with the RKO and Monogram film libraries and UA corporate records, United Artists created a truly great resource for the study of American film. Acquired by United Artists in 1957, during a period when the major studios sold off their films for use on television, the Warner library is by far the richest portion of the gift, containing eight hundred sound features, fifteen hundred short subjects, nineteen thousand still negatives, legal files, and press books, in addition to screenplays for the bulk of the Warner Brothers product from 1930 to 1950. For the purposes of this project, the company has granted the Center whatever publication rights it holds to the Warner films. In so doing, UA has provided the Center another opportunity to advance the cause of film scholarship.

Our goal in publishing these Warner Brothers screenplays is to explicate the art of screenwriting during the thirties and forties, the so-called Golden Age of Hollywood. In preparing a critical introduction and annotating the screenplay, the editor of each volume is asked to cover such topics as the development of the screenplay from its source to the final shooting script, differences between the final shooting script and the release print, production information, exploitation and critical reception of the film, its historical importance, its directorial style, and its position within the genre. He is also encouraged to go beyond these guidelines to incorporate supplemental information concerning the studio system of motion picture production.

We could set such an ambitious goal because of the richness of the script files in the Warner Film Library. For many film titles, the files might contain the property (novel, play, short story, or original idea), research materials, variant drafts of scripts (from story outline to treatment to shooting script), post-production items such as press books and dialogue continuities, and legal records (details of the acquisition of the property, copyright registration, and contracts with actors and directors). Editors of the Wisconsin/Warner Bros. Screenplay Series receive copies of all the materials, along with prints of the films (the most authoritative ones available for reference purposes), to use in preparing the introductions and annotating the final shooting scripts.

In the process of preparing the screenplays for publication, typographical errors were corrected, punctuation and capitalization were modernized, and the format was redesigned to facilitate readability.

Unless otherwise specified, the photographs are frame enlargements taken from a 35-mm print of the film provided by United Artists.

In theory, the Center should have received the extant scripts of all pre-1951 Warner Brothers productions when the United Artists Collection was established. Recent events, however, have created at least some doubt in this area. Late in 1977, Warners donated collections consisting of the company's production records and distribution records to the University of Southern California and Princeton University respectively. The precise contents of the collections are not known, since at the present time they are not generally open to scholars. To the best of our knowledge, all extant scripts have been considered in the preparation of these volumes. Should any other versions be discovered at a later date, we will recognize them in future printings of any volumes so affected.

Tino Balio
General Editor

Introduction: *In Search of Happiness*

Arthur Hove

The gold digger as a species of opportunist first entered the American lexicon with the opening of a Broadway comedy at the Lyceum theater on the evening of September 30, 1919.[1] Alexander Woollcott found *The Gold Diggers* to be "an unexpectedly conventional play about a great-hearted chorus girl—screamingly funny at times and rather dull at others."[2] The focus throughout the play is on character. The story is a familiar one, dealing with the fortunes of a group of young women who have come to New York with the usual hopes of achieving stardom in the theater. In keeping with theatrical convention, the girls in the play are a diverse lot, similar in many ways to that archetypal squad of soldiers one is forever encountering in war novels and films. Yet, despite their diversity, the girls share a common interest—finding well-heeled men who can be separated from their money.

A good portion of the play's action, which is centered exclusively in a New York City apartment, is spent revealing the personalities of the young women. The three principals are familiar

---

1. Produced by David Belasco, *The Gold Diggers* was written by Avery Hopwood, a journeyman playwright who, following graduation from the University of Michigan, began his career as a reporter on his hometown newspaper, the *Cleveland Plain Dealer*, before moving to Broadway. Hopwood wrote a large number of plays, usually in collaboration with other authors—the most noted being Mary Roberts Rinehart. Some of his once popular efforts include *The Girl in the Limousine*, *Getting Gertie's Garter*, *The Demi-Virgin*, *Little Miss Bluebeard*, and *Naughty Cinderella*. Even though he was highly successful and prolific, most of his plays are now forgotten or seldom revived. Hopwood died at age fifty-four in July 1928 while swimming in the sea at Juan-les-Pins on the French Riviera.

2. *New York Times*, October 1, 1919.

types: the well-traveled cynic (Mabel), the ingenue (Violet), and the professional artiste (Jerry). The ingenue is in love with a wholesome, good-looking young man (Wally). The two want to get married but must first obtain the consent of Wally's guardian, his Uncle Stephen. The situation is further compounded by the threat of Wally's losing his five-million-dollar inheritance if he marries without permission. Stephen is something of a straight-laced Boston aristocrat (characterized as an "old prune") who is trying to protect his nephew from falling victim to the wiles of callow chorus girls.

Believing that nothing should serve as an impediment to the marriage of true minds, Jerry prepares aggressively to find a way to alter Stephen's stuffily provincial view of the world. She intends to force him to agree to Wally and Violet's marriage by making Stephen believe it is she whom Wally wants to marry. This ruse involves her temporarily assuming Violet's identity, if in name only.

Stephen, in the meantime, seeks the assistance of the family lawyer (Blake). It is Blake who, in dispensing advice, delineates the characteristics of the species identified in the play's title: "A gold digger is a woman, generally young, who extracts money and other valuables from the gentlemen of her acquaintance, usually without making them any adequate return." (His counterpart in the film, Faneuil H. Peabody, offers a supplementary definition: "All women of the theater are chiselers, parasites, or—as we called them—gold diggers.") ·

Blake's libido is stronger than his advice. Before long, he and Mabel are a duo. Blake begins to enjoy himself, falling victim to Mabel the gold digger. At the same time, Jerry is making every effort to embarrass Uncle Stephen. She becomes assertively manic to give Stephen and Blake the impression that all chorus girls are just what those two presume them to be. Stephen, however, finds her actions and her personality "refreshingly natural." He begins to fall for her. And she for him. He asks Jerry to marry him, but she has become so intent in trying to prove that chorus girls can be noble that she overplays her hand and feels embarrassed about her excesses.

Stephen offers forgiveness. He has come to realize that chorus girls are people: "Now that I've got to really know them, I've found out that most of them are nice, hard-working girls." He further demonstrates his newly found enlightenment by giving his formal blessing to the Wally/Violet marriage. As the play closes, Stephen and Jerry reach an understanding and Mabel has Blake in harness.

The moral of the story is that chorus girls really do have hearts of gold; they are not just floozies whose major ambition is to acquire as much as they can in the shortest time possible.

Warners had twice transferred the Hopwood play to film before 1933 with a silent version in 1923 and a talking version in 1929. The latter—*Gold Diggers of Broadway*—did not represent a significant departure from Hopwood's play; Hopwood, in fact, had a hand in the script, which was written by Robert Lord. However, this film, directed by Roy Del Ruth, did offer a new dimension beyond the fact that it was a talkie: it was a musical and was shot in "100% Natural Color."[3] Its principal star was Winnie Lightner, an actress who appeared in several other films in the early 1930s but dropped out of sight and sound as the decade matured.

The film contained two songs by Al Dubin and Joe Burke that have endured to be resurrected periodically: "Painting the Clouds with Sunshine" and "Tip-toe thru' the Tulips with Me." *New York Times* critic Mordaunt Hall described the film as "an extraordinarily pleasing entertainment" (August 31, 1929).

At this time, when talking pictures were becoming a nationwide commonplace, the movie musical experienced its first major period of popularity. As Miles Kreuger has noted, 1929 "was a year obsessed with musicals: light ones, farcical ones, operettas,

3. It is not clear what the studio meant by "100% Natural Color." *New York Times* critic Mordaunt Hall said that the film took every opportunity "of the Technicolor process in producing the hue and glitter of a musical comedy" (August 31, 1929). Although colored motion picture film had been in use since before the turn of the century when film was colored by hand, two-color processes involving various image-splitting techniques were most commonly used in the first three decades of this century. Technicolor, which added dye images of cyan (blue-green), magenta, and yellow to a black-and-white "key" image, began to gain wide use in the 1930s. See "The Development of Colour Cinematography" in Roger Manvell, ed., *The International Encyclopedia of Film* (New York: Crown, 1972), pp. 29–48.

tear-jerkers with songs, revues without a plot, all were fair game."[4]

The biggest movie of the year was MGM's *The Broadway Melody*. Two important directors who got their start at the time and who made musicals that broke away from the conventions of the theater and music hall to explore the artistic possibilities of film were Ernst Lubitsch and Rouben Mamoulian. Lubitsch's films—particularly *The Love Parade* (1929) and *The Smiling Lieutenant* (1931)—utilized the visual appeal and singing talents of Jeanette MacDonald and Maurice Chevalier. John Russell Taylor has characterized Lubitsch's films as "light, fast and sophisticated, using to the full the cinema's ability to cut corners in plotting and reduce everything to essentials."[5]

The early musicals were heavily populated by stars who adapted with reasonable ease to the new medium. Many were former vaudevillians: Chevalier, Eddie Cantor, Al Jolson, Fannie Brice, the Marx Brothers, Sophie Tucker, George M. Cohan, and Jimmy Durante. Others were ingenues whose popularity reached its zenith at the time (Janet Gaynor, Marion Davies, Marilyn Miller, Helen Morgan, Lillian Roth, Bebe Daniels) or whose influence would increase as the public developed new ideas about how leading ladies should look and act (Joan Crawford, Norma Shearer, Jeanette MacDonald, Ginger Rogers, Marlene Dietrich, and Claudette Colbert).

Leading men were represented by Chevalier, Adolphe Menjou, Walter Pidgeon, Rudy Vallee, Conrad Nagel, Lawrence Tibbett, Douglas Fairbanks (both junior and senior), and Buddy Rogers. The clowns, those solid second bananas, were present too—Jack Oakie, Buster Keaton, Harry Richman, Edward Everett Horton, Jack Haley, Frank Morgan, and Victor Moore.

At first, the public eagerly accepted the novelty of the musical and its invariable "galaxy of stars." These "stars," however, were unable to carry otherwise ponderous and unimaginative films with the sheer force of their personalities and talents. The public's appetite for musicals was soon sated. After an initial surge, pro-

4. Miles Kreuger, ed., *The Movie Musical: From Vitaphone to 42nd Street* (New York: Dover, 1975), p. 11.

5. John Russell Taylor and Arthur Jackson, *The Hollywood Musical* (London: Secker & Warburg, 1976), p. 16.

duction dwindled rapidly. As the 1930s began, the Hollywood studios made substantial cutbacks in their production of musicals. The Depression was deepening and people's minds were temporarily elsewhere.

The eclipse of the musical lasted from 1930 through 1932. By 1933, the musical was revived in a sudden and dramatic way with the appearance of *42nd Street*, a Warner Brothers film that utilized the backstage convention that had made *The Broadway Melody* so popular. Warners had initiated work on *Gold Diggers* even before *42nd Street* appeared in January 1933 and became a surprise success.

It was obvious that Warners was taking a gamble, playing a long-shot hunch by putting two musicals into production at a time when the future of the film musical was uncertain. In the case of *Gold Diggers*, the financial success of the 1929 version seemed motivation enough to try again with a new story and cast.[6]

Development of the Screenplay

In a memo to Lucien Hubbard, the film's supervisor, producer Darryl F. Zanuck announced in November 1932 that Erwin Gelsey had been assigned "to adapt *Golddiggers of 1933* under the temporary title of 'High Life.'" Zanuck explained he wanted to retain as much of the 1929 version as possible, "especially the great comedy sequences; however, I know we can improve the dialogue and smarten up the situations and, of course, we will not do nearly so many musical numbers as we did before."

Secrecy was important. "The main thing we want to do," Zanuck said, "is keep this quiet and not let anyone know what we are working on as when we come out with the announcement later on, I want it to be made like a big news break."

It is obvious that Warners wanted to move quickly from story outline to shooting script. Gelsey, who was joined by James Sey-

---

6. "Such was the success of this [1929] picture that complainant determined to produce a new talking motion picture version of the play under the title 'Gold Diggers of 1933.'" From an appeal filed with the U.S. Court of Appeals for the Second Circuit in New York. See page 22 for the reason for and the context of this legal action.

mour on the project, submitted a treatment at the end of November. Gelsey and Seymour began with the instructions that they should be concerned primarily with the updating of the earlier play and film versions of *Gold Diggers*. In a joint memo to Hubbard that accompanied their rough outline for "High Life," they noted: "While, in our opinion, this can be developed as an amusing farce, the story does not seem to us to justify a big and expensive all-star musical production."

Despite Zanuck's instructions and their expressed doubts about the all-star musical, the Gelsey and Seymour outline provided for the insertion of musical numbers. Its primary focus, however, is to identify characters similar to the three pairings of women and men who form the principal interest in the Hopwood play and to lay out the plot line of confused identity and the triumph of true love over adversity.

The early treatments list the names of actresses and actors (Tallulah Bankhead, George Brent, Charles Winninger, Bebe Daniels, Glenda Farrell, Pat O'Brien) in order to suggest character types. The names in the outline point to a common Warner Brothers practice of the time, one that was to have even greater influence at MGM in the 1940s. The studio maintained a stock company of stars who were available on short notice. Most of them played representative character types, and they generally enjoyed relatively equal billing so that no single star completely dominated the billboard for a given picture. Their presence in the background made it possible to create or tailor a screenplay to take into account the qualities a particular star could bring to a role. The screenwriters simply inserted the name of an actor or actress to indicate what they had in mind, thereby saving time in presenting the details of a character in an early treatment.

In addition to featuring comedy and music, *Gold Diggers* was to be a vehicle for showcasing the talents of members of the Warner Brothers stable who would generate interest and excitement among the anticipated audience.

The initial outline of the basic story and its important elements was followed by a skeleton outline that further developed the translation of the story to film. The outline becomes a specific listing of the scenes and the visual transitions that can be expected to form the major sequences of the film.

The script materials for *Gold Diggers* (see Inventory) show that things seemed to follow in a natural, orderly process. A revised treatment makes a few changes in the beginning and in various points within the general story, but the overall concept seems to be accepted. Lucien Hubbard makes some comments in the margin of a draft of the revised treatment, finding one segment "too similar to *42nd Street*," and another "too extreme," and points out that one section "all seems phony." But his comments appear as editorial observations rather than a questioning of the basic concept of the film.

Then, two days before Christmas of 1932, a new treatment of "High Life" appears. Gelsey's name is gone from the title page. The script is now by David Boehm and James Seymour. The story has been altered. The reason for the sudden and substantial revision is unclear, particularly when everyone seems to be in a hurry to begin production to hold to Zanuck's plans to "produce the picture the latter part of December."

The new treatment contains some major changes in character concepts, changes that give emphasis to new characters who are mutations of those found in the play and earlier film versions. One of the strong plot lines is still here—how to put on a show in a period of financial hard times—but the interrelationships between various characters have become more complex, to the point of being unwieldy. For example, Aline MacMahon is no longer conceived of as Trixie the jaded show girl, but "a blue-blooded Boston aristocrat of about forty—the high-bred, stiff-necked, wealthy widow of a stodgy New York banker of the old school." Ruby Keeler is her maid/companion. George Brent (Warren William in the film) is a "hard-headed, conservative businessman. . . . His position in banking circles is dominant and invulnerable." His younger brother, Dick Powell, is afraid of him: "When he talks of his brother, he is like a frightened child."

Additional characters appear on the scene. The names of Pat O'Brien, Bebe Daniels, Charles Winninger, Claire Dodd, and Guy Kibbee are added to the roster of stars, and the connections established between them in the story become so involved that the scenario eventually seems like something describing a family reunion of the Medicis.

The treatment has become so complex by now that nothing is going to work. The audience simply will not be able to keep the characters straight—no matter how well known the star playing a particular role. A simpler framework is needed.

Less than a month later, Seymour and Boehm check in again with a Revised Temporary shooting script. It follows the Gelsey and Seymour outlines and is the first draft of a script combining dialogue by Boehm. Symmetry has returned to the relationships between the characters, and we have dramatic tension functioning on two levels: (1) in the relationships between the three principal couples (Brad and Polly, J. Lawrence and Carol, and Peabody and Trixie), and (2) in the efforts Barney Hopkins is making to mount a new show in the face of economic uncertainty. There is the obviously growing acknowledgment by the writers that musical production numbers will be a significant part of the film. They have begun to build them into the script. Also, by this time a substantial portion of the script has been given over to the business involved with putting on a musical—the backstage convention that was initiated in 1929 with *The Broadway Melody* and revived in *42nd Street*.

Although there is a caution at the beginning of this version ("This script is not final and is given to you for advance information only"), it is obvious that the decision has been made to follow closely the story line of the Hopwood play. The title of this version is still "High Life," but the content is *Gold Diggers*.

A line in this draft appropriately describes the function of the screenwriters in this particular enterprise. It is spoken by Fay (Ginger Rogers), who is telling about her work in a drugstore. "And among my responsibilities," she explains, "is dispensing concoctions of syrup and soda." *Gold Diggers of 1933* is a concoction of something sweet and bubbly, something that tingles on the palate, tastes good as it goes down, but ultimately has very little staying power.

The Revised Final or actual shooting script (the version printed in this volume) appeared on February 8, 1933, less than a month after the revised temporary was being considered. Ben Markson's name joins those of Seymour and Boehm on the script, which is now titled *Gold Diggers of 1933*. Gelsey's name does not appear on this version, but the screen credits list him and Seymour as being responsible for the screenplay while Boehm and Markson are given credit for the dialogue. The songs were written by Al Dubin (lyrics) and Harry Warren (music), two men who worked together on several Warners films.

As indicated above, Dubin had teamed with Joe Burke on the 1929 *Gold Diggers* film. Warren and Dubin had collaborated on *42nd Street*, producing two songs that have been remembered: "You're Getting to be a Habit with Me" and "Shuffle off to Buffalo." In the 1935 *Gold Diggers* film (starring Dick Powell, Adolphe Menjou, Hugh Herbert, and Glenda Farrell), they introduced "The Lullaby of Broadway," a song that has become a kind of Tin Pan Alley anthem.

Harry Warren was a prolific composer who managed to adapt his songs to changing tastes and changing film styles. Among his still popular numbers are "I'll String along with You," "The More I See You," "Chattanooga Choo-Choo," "Serenade in Blue," and "This Heart of Mine." In addition to Dubin, his collaborators included Mack Gordon and Johnny Mercer.

Since the Revised Final script shows February 1933 dates and the film was reviewed in New York early in June 1933, it appears as though producer, directors, cast, and stagehands were virtually waiting on the sound stage for the script to come out of the typewriter. The film's press book reinforces the haste to follow up on the by now demonstrated success of *42nd Street*. Theater managers were instructed to "make sure the public understands this new hit is from Warner Bros., the same company that gave them *42nd Street* and not an imitation from another company. . . . Get over the additional fact that it has very many of the same stars and chorus beauties they enjoyed so much in *42nd Street*, and is the work of the same composers, artists, designers, etc."

Production (the film was shot in forty-five days) must have involved both a logistic and artistic frenzy—particularly with two directors: Mervyn LeRoy for the story and Busby Berkeley for the musical numbers.

When the dialogue transcript and the actual scenes in the film are compared with the shooting script published here, it is obvious that the script was tinkered with as the filming progressed. However, no real violence has been done to the story line or the overall concept of the film. The most noticeable difference between the script and the film is the omission of several passages of dialogue, which is of little consequence. The extra dialogue does not further establish character or explain any particular aspect of the story. It is generally gratuitous material. It performs the same function it did in Hopwood's loquacious play—to give us an additional look at how really clever the gold diggers are. Perhaps the extra dialogue was necessary and helpful on the stage, but the musical numbers accomplish the same thing in the film. Its consequent impact on the running time of the film would only slow things down. The film's quick pace has been a major factor in its sustained appeal over the years.

The script for *Gold Diggers of 1933* is the product of a group of Hollywood wordsmiths hired to put together something that could be filmed quickly, something to take advantage of a particular time when it was (rightly) assumed that such a film would attract a large audience. The plot involves the simultaneous balancing of characters and interweaving of story lines. The stories involving the development of the various characters are handled well, but the film is little more than a commonplace variation on the boy-meets-girl theme that has been with us since the romances of the Middle Ages.

The dialogue in the script is sometimes topical, but invariably fresh. It retains its freshness through a certain sarcasm and spunkiness. Much of the film's continuing appeal, of course, is related to the skills of the directors and the players who have given the film an added dimension through their ability to radiate an innocence and enthusiasm that is infectious.

The Two Directors

If one wants to understand how a film is put together, this script is valuable in providing an illustration of the practical concerns essential to the process. Studying the script and seeing the film, one realizes how far writers can go before the baton is passed to the director. This film provides an additional wrinkle because of its two directors. LeRoy, as we can see, was the one most bound by the integrity of the script. Berkeley had a greater opportunity to let his imagination take flight, to soar into those realms of high-stepping folderol that became his trademark. Berkeley's numbers provide an augmentation that certainly makes the film more appealing. Without the story, however, the musical numbers would be meaningless fragments, a visual tutti-frutti with no reason for being other than to show off the director's imagination and skill.

Unlike many other musicals, the reality of this film is that the story line can stand on its own without undue embellishment. The film script has improved on the Hopwood play, making it tighter and eliminating those periods of dullness that troubled Alexander Woollcott. Much of the original play contained long blocks of dialogue designed to reveal the personalities and life histories of the various characters. Gimmicks added a quaintness to extract a laugh from the audience. One of the characters, for example, is an aging show girl who is losing her looks and is forced to supplement her income by selling soap. This situation contributes nothing to the plot but is used as a hackneyed laugh-getter throughout the play.

At two points in the play, so many characters are on the stage that a diagram is supplied as part of the stage direction to show where everyone would be placed. Finally, the play is riddled with colloquialisms designed to illustrate how thoroughly contemporary the show girls are. This argot is now almost indecipherable without extensive glossing.

Mervyn LeRoy obviously recognized that if the play were simply transferred to the screen, it would generate boredom rather than enthusiasm. As a result, large chunks of dialogue that appear in the final script are not in the film. The insertion of the musical numbers may account for the cuts, but it is more apparent that the pieces that have been eliminated do not lessen understanding or effectiveness.

LeRoy wanted this film to be "grander" than the 1929 version of *Gold Diggers*. To be grander meant to be more filmic and less stagelike. LeRoy's contribution to the effort was to keep the action moving. Berkeley's numbers, which LeRoy described as "some of the most memorable moments in his [Berkeley's] illustrious career,"[7] brought a visual opulence to the production.

Gold Diggers of 1933 works well as a film because of a strong symbiotic relationship between the two directors. LeRoy's technique in the narrative sequences complements Berkeley's numbers. The song and dance routines evolve naturally out of the narrative segments, assisted by the backstage musical convention. As a result, there are no obvious and insurmountable differences between the two components of the film.

LeRoy sustains an effective balance between pace and design. At the beginning and in subsequent portions of the film when quick-cutting is needed to set the scene, he uses montage to move quickly through time. When more time is needed to develop character rather than simply set the scene, there is a well-modulated juxtaposition of close-ups and medium and long shots. This alternation allows us to consider the characters as individuals in their own right rather than as two-dimensional cardboard cutouts of show business stereotypes.

Throughout the film, LeRoy's camera consistently offers vignettes that give us a quick and memorable glance at character: Dick Powell's winsomeness, Guy Kibbee's alternating sternness and foolishness, Warren William's haughty dourness, Aline MacMahon's knowingness, Ruby Keeler's fecklessness, and Joan Blondell's verve.

The frame enlargements included in this volume demonstrate how well the two directors complement each other. Their regard for the importance of carefully composed shots gives the film a unified visual texture. LeRoy's camera does not move around as much as Berkeley's, but it is seldom out of place or in a position that seems unnatural to the action of any given scene.

The overall effectiveness of LeRoy's work, when contrasted with Berkeley's, is less obvious. The sheer visual pyrotechnics of Berkeley's choreography call attention to the so-called brilliance

7. Mervyn LeRoy, as told to Dick Kleiner, *Mervyn LeRoy: Take One* (New York: Hawthorn, 1974), p. 119.

of the director. His style, as a result, has been analyzed, commented upon, and imitated to the point of saturation. Its most obvious features depend on costumes, props, pulchritude, and geometry.

Berkeley's camera is consistently on the move, becoming a part of the choreography itself. He is invariably setting up for a boom shot, a tracking shot, or an overhead shot. The effect is kaleidoscopic—in the sense that a kaleidoscope when rotated yields new patterns, new surprises with each turn.

Berkeley's approach is ultimately a stylistic dead end, however. Eventually one wonders how many variations on a theme there can be. While the patterns in a kaleidoscope mathematically approach infinity, the designs we see there seldom retain our interest for very long. In order to seem fresh and original, Berkeley constantly searched for one more surprising visual variation, one more gimmick to tantalize the eye. The ultimate outcome is that his work could not help but contain a strong element of self-parody.

The synthesis resulting from the work of the two directors is a film with a fundamental honesty. Perhaps this quality is best reflected by the players. They are so unguardedly wholesome in their appearance that they match the description that Stephen (J. Lawrence in the film) uses in the Hopwood play—"so refreshingly natural."

There is a luminescent quality about the stars, an innocence that is infectious as well as convincing. Ruby Keeler, Dick Powell, Joan Blondell, and Ginger Rogers are extremely attractive people who radiate a vitality that both LeRoy and Berkeley used to its fullest advantage. It is a quality that travels well, a quality that, when combined with the solid architecture of the film, gives it a freshness that remains, even though the environment of society has changed considerably in the meantime.

LeRoy summarizes the essence that he tried to relate: "For me always, the sole criterion for selecting a film was that it had a good, solid story and that it had the quality I call 'heart.' "[8]

8. LeRoy, *Mervyn LeRoy*, p. 180.

Introduction

In the Money

The opening number of *Gold Diggers of 1933* features a precisely marching platoon of chorus girls (headed by Ginger Rogers) decked out in coin costumes. "The Gold Diggers' Song" ("We're in the Money") is designed to give cheer to a beleaguered citizenry that had gone through four years of economic depression and was looking for some indication of a change of fortune, some assurance that

> The long lost dollar has come back to the fold—
> With silver you can turn your dreams to gold . . .

In a deeper sense, the number is indicative of the film's value to Warner Brothers. Something about Avery Hopwood's conception of the show girl with a heart—and soul—has an appeal that has now extended through several generations of American entertainment.

From the outset, there was gold in the gold digger concept. The property was worth fighting for—so much so that in 1934 Warner Brothers secured an injunction against Majestic Pictures Corporation and Capital Film Exchange, Inc., to forbid them "from distributing, exhibiting or advertising a talking motion picture under the title *Gold Diggers of Paris*, or under any title containing the words 'Gold Diggers.' "[9]

In 1933 Majestic and Capital had made the film *Gold Diggers of Paris*, which Warners contended had characters similar to those in the Hopwood play and was intended "to capitalize the good will and reputation" of Warner Brothers through the association of the Majestic/Capital film with the Hopwood play. Warners also pointed out that it had purchased exclusive rights to Hopwood's play from David Belasco for a 1923 silent film and a subsequent 1929 talking version. The result, Warners maintained, was that the public had come to associate films based on the Hopwood play with Warner Brothers Pictures, Inc.; people would make the logical assumption that Warners, and not Majestic/Capital, had produced *Gold Diggers*

9. The major portion of the economic data in this section is from the appeal cited in footnote 6.

in Paris—this virtually simultaneous with the release of *Gold Diggers of 1933*.

The stakes in this battle over the right to exclusivity were obviously high. The Hopwood play ran on Broadway for 90 successive weeks following its September 1919 opening. On tour throughout the United States it logged 528 performances from 1921 through 1923. During this time, the play grossed more than $1.9 million. The 1923 silent film grossed $470,000. The first talking version cost $725,000 to produce—a good proportion of the expense no doubt was linked to the cost of producing the film in color. The expense was obviously worthwhile, as the film grossed more than $2.5 million in the United States and Canada. An additional $1.3 million was grossed from exhibition of the film in other locations around the world.

From this record there is no question that Warners had more than a passing interest in maintaining exclusive rights to the property. *Gold Diggers of 1933*, which was produced at an approximate cost of $300,000, was expected to be a money-maker—something that would bankroll further ventures into the musical field; all the more reason to seek the injunction.

When the injunction was granted, Warners, in a further effort to make sure its *Gold Diggers* investment potential was secure, paid the New York corporation of Hopwood Plays, Inc., the sum of $7,500 for the "sole and exclusive and complete right in perpetuity to use the title 'The Gold Diggers' and/or any variations thereof" for commercial entertainment properties ranging from silent pictures to radio and television.[10]

Warners' promotion of the 1933 film was elaborate, extensive, and in keeping with the hoopla that *42nd Street* had initiated. The press books demonstrate that the studio intended to dictate the way that theaters would advertise this film and others produced at the time. It helped, of course, to have your own chain of theaters, as Warner Brothers did.

Using the *42nd Street* formula, Warners laid it on thick for *Gold*

10. From an agreement reached between Hopwood Plays, Inc., and J. J. Schwebel and Warner Bros. Pictures, Inc., New York City, December 16, 1939.

Diggers. The instructions to theater managers were to "make sure the public understands this new hit is from Warner Bros., the same company that gave them *42nd Street,* and not an imitation from another company."

The promotion actually began before the film had gone into production. The chorus of two hundred girls seen in the film was supposedly handpicked by Busby Berkeley. The selections were made from ten thousand entries in a national search. The process used is described in the press book: "The initial selections were made in Warner Bros. theatres throughout the country. The most promising of the candidates who presented themselves were then sent to Warner Bros. Studios in North Hollywood, where they were sorted out until 1,000 were left. The thousand beauties were then segregated and given tasks and gradually eliminated until the required two hundred were picked." The reported selection was catholic. "No one standard of beauty was used. The girls represent every ideal of beauty—pulchritude to suit every taste. There are blondes, brunettes and red heads, tall girls and short girls, slim girls and plump girls, peppy girls and languid girls, but each and every one with personality."

One has to be skeptical about all this hype. Two hundred beauties on a sound stage at once would look more like a massed company front of marching soldiers than a crisply stepping platoon of pulchritude (unless, of course, different combinations were selected to dance in the various numbers and no girl danced in more than one number). Another source of doubt is the economics involved in transporting, housing, and feeding all those girls, girls, girls to provide the *corps de ballet* for the film.

The Depression public did not seem concerned about truth in advertising. Obviously, it was not a concern of Warners, judging from the other devices used to attract attention to the film: a special ballyhoo record with songs from the picture that could be played on the local radio station; a ten-chapter newspaper serialization of the film story "from the graphic pen of the celebrated Hollywood writer Carlisle Jones"; a dramatic reading to be done by members of the local drama society or "artists at the radio station"; a silhouette contest featuring identifications of the major stars; a scenic float for "street ballyhoo"; a chain letter; a lobby peep show; chocolate and aluminum coins to be used as an advertising giveaway; doorknob hangers advertising the film; and a large variety of cutouts and posters of the principal players.

After *Gold Diggers of 1933*, the idea began to show signs of suffering from overexploitation. The subsequent uses of the general theme became attenuated efforts to capitalize on the success of the 1933 film. *Gold Diggers of 1935, of 1938,* and *in Paris* (1938) did not have the vitality of the original to sustain the public's interest. As is so often the case, a good idea had been beaten to death with a stick. In this case, the vein of gold simply petered out.

Still, attempts to revive the concept surface periodically. *Painting the Clouds with Sunshine* (1951) was a feeble reworking of the idea that took its title from a song in the 1929 version. It starred Dennis Morgan and Virginia Mayo and shifted the scene from New York to Las Vegas. The most recent reincarnation occurred with the 1968 television show "Dean Martin Presents the Golddiggers." This time there was little effort to make a story out of anything. The updated gold diggers were recruits from a Las Vegas chorus line who sang and danced in reasonable unison, but had little more to do on camera than stimulate the hormones of the male viewers in the audience.

Happiness in Hard Times

In analyzing *Gold Diggers of 1933* in its social context, some critics have tended to see the film as an allegorical representation of the forces that produced the Great Depression. Russell Campbell and Michael Roth, writing in a special issue of *The Velvet Light Trap* devoted to an assessment of "Warner Brothers in the Thirties" (June 1971), have made some useful observations about the sociopolitical aspects of the Depression and their influences on the films of the period.

As Campbell notes, "Warners was the only studio to feature working class characters with any regularity. Shop girls, bellhops, linen girls, barbers, stenographers, taxi drivers were presented convincingly, without any condescension (indeed, the preoccupations of their social betters were normally satirized). Businessmen were repeatedly attacked as exploitative or corrupt" (p. 3).

Michael Roth sees the "archetypal Warners musical" as "a precursor and product of the optimism-in-the-midst-of-depression created by FDR" (p. 20). He scratches further below the surface as he notes, "The Depression not only raised questions about the viability of American capitalism, but also called into question the ethos and mythology which was both the product and support of that system. Musicals and crime films were the two major film genres to explore this crisis." Roth further notes that "the Warners musical of the early 1930s tried to come to terms with the questioning of the American Dream and to reaffirm faith in that ideal" (p. 21).

It is not unexpected, therefore, for Roth to conclude that "rather than being 'escapist' in any sense it seems to me that the great Warners musicals are essentially political. Basic to the collectivist nature of these musicals is their ritualized form. The quintessential symbol is the Berkeley dance number. The urge of the dances and the films is towards cooperation and collective effort. Individually, Berkeley's dancers would amount to little. When, as he occasionally does, Berkeley isolates chorus girls with the camera, or has their faces follow each other filling the screen, the dances are least effective and border on being foolish" (p. 25).

Stanley Solomon regards the motivation of the characters of *Gold Diggers of 1933* as being more elemental. He sees the central problem as one of basic economic survival—throughout the film "money looms as an obsession, poverty as an ever-present threat."[11]

Andrew Bergman offers another perspective. He says quite bluntly of this and similar films, "Of course, they were escapist— a nation could drown its sorrows in legs and glitter, and plumes and teeth and sweet harmonizing."[12]

Entertainment or polemic? Or both? The answer invariably hinges on one's biases. It also is related to a crucial question involving the analysis of any film. The documents available in the Warner Brothers files suggest the advisability of taking a pragmatic view when assessing the intent of the producers. Two fac-

11. Stanley J. Solomon, *Beyond Formula: American Film Genres* (New York: Harcourt Brace Jovanovich, 1976), p. 80.

12. Andrew Bergman, *We're in the Money: Depression America and Its Films* (New York: Harper & Row, 1971), p. 64.

tors support this approach: (1) the proven financial potential of the *Gold Diggers* property and (2) the script and the various treatments leading up to the production of the film.

The overriding consideration in the treatments and script drafts is to put together a film that will capture the imagination of a public looking for a few moments of release and entertainment. There is virtually no sign of gathering ammunition to shoot holes in the American capitalist system, a system that some critics presume to be corrupt because it derives its strength from exploiting the working man.

Most references to capitalism as an economic-political determinant in the film are incidental. The early script treatments are entitled "High Life." "Low Life" would have been a more appropriate title for those seeking to make a case against the evils of capitalism.

The key piece of evidence for presuming the film is political (and ultimately Marxist) is the "Forgotten Man" number. The lyrics of this number appear unceremoniously as scene 84 of the shooting script and are wedged into the business establishing Brad's true identity. The plan was to close with a reprise of "Shadow Waltz" and "We're in the Money." The only other reference to the number appears in scene 45 when Brad says he has a tune, "Remember My Forgotten Man," but *no words yet.* He has simply been moved to write something as a tribute to the men he has seen standing in a bread line on Times Square waiting for a handout because they can't get jobs.

Barney Hopkins, responding to the cue from Brad, exclaims: "That's just what this show's about—the Depression—men marching—marching in the rain—marching—marching—doughnuts and crullers—jobs—jobs—marching—marching—marching in the rain—and in the background will be Carol—spirit of the Depression—a blue song—no, not a blue song—but a wailing—a wailing—and this woman—this gorgeous woman—singing this number that tears your heart out—the big parade—the big parade of tears—"

Barney's hyperbole is misleading and Ned Sparks's delivery of this little homily is hardly convincing in terms of his commitment to promoting social justice. Also, from what we see of Barney's

Broadway production in the film, the Depression may provide a context, but it certainly is not the primary focus. The name of Barney's show, as it appears on the theater marquee, is *Forgotten Melody*, something that sounds more romantic than polemic. The two numbers ("Pettin' in the Park" and "Shadow Waltz") in Barney's show that precede "My Forgotten Man" are puff pieces that have no biting edge whatsoever. They are primarily decorative and designed to "capitalize" on the obvious physical appeal of Dick Powell, Ruby Keeler, and the sumptuous Berkeley *corps de ballet*. These numbers are hardly the stuff that provides a trenchant commentary on the evils of American capitalism.

The lyrics of "Remember My Forgotten Man" reveal further ambiguities. The film version of the song begins in uncertainty, not knowing for sure if the Forgotten Man "deserves a bit of sympathy." Carol, who is singing the song, seems to be searching more for personal security than for a means to serve up an indictment of the capitalist system:

> . . . ever since the world began—
> A woman's got to have a man
> Forgetting him, you see, means
> You're forgetting me.

Taken in the context of what has apparently gone before in Barney's show, the "Forgotten Man" number is incongruous. In a Revised Temporary version of the film script, the number was called "Carol's Blues," appeared in the approximate middle of the film, and used a shot of the Bonus Army marching in the background.[13] Another reference labels it a "torch" song. Upon exami-

---

13. The Bonus Army was composed of approximately seventeen thousand World War I veterans from all sections of the country who marched and hitchhiked to Washington, D.C., in late May of 1932. The army camped in jerry-built shacks within sight of the Capitol and mounted an effort to encourage Congress to provide them with a full and immediate payment of the veterans' bonuses due them by Constitutional mandate. Most of the army disbanded in June when Congress voted down their request, but two thousand remained on and had to be forcibly removed by Regular Army troops on orders from President Hoover. Two of the officers participating in the action were Douglas MacArthur and Dwight D. Eisenhower.

nation of its content and placement in the film, it appears to be an afterthought—something to salve the producers' consciences or to furnish a footnote to the general social context in which the film was made.

The business immediately preceding the number is hardly designed to prepare the audience for a "message." Polly and Brad have been married. So have Trixie and Peabody. J. Lawrence and Carol are obviously headed for the altar. In a moment of magnanimity, J. Lawrence tells Brad that he and Polly can have the ten thousand dollars Trixie extracted from him earlier as a wedding present. Happy endings are in order for everyone—even Barney, whose current show is a success and certainly will provide him enough revenue to produce another one. As happiness radiates around the music hall, Carol goes into the totally incongruous "Forgotten Man" number.

Examining the characters of the film, one cannot detect any exploitative capitalists lurking in the wings. The only people with any money are J. Lawrence, Peabody, and Brad. J. Lawrence is hardly a titan of industry who ruthlessly tinkers with people's lives as he fights for profits. Instead, he is a stuffed shirt who is custodian of his family's apparently considerable fortune. Brad is the second son who feels none of the family pressures that shape the attitudes of his older brother. Brad seems perfectly content pursuing a career in music rather than getting caught up in the dullness of managing his family's money. Peabody is a teddy bear of a man who has made his own fortune by advising others how to hang onto theirs. These are not Andrew Carnegie or John D. Rockefeller types. They would not raise the eyebrows of muckrakers Ida Tarbell, Lincoln Steffens, or Upton Sinclair. John Dos Passos would have found them too bland to bother satirizing. J. Lawrence, Brad, and Peabody are guilty of no known crime; they just have more money than most people and maintain a somewhat narrow view of the world—the latter misdemeanor being far from the exclusive province of the rich.

The have-nots of the film present no sharp contrasts. Barney has no money of his own, but he spends most of his waking moments trying to extract funds from others so he can produce his shows.

He is not obsessed with raising money to give away to the poor and downtrodden. The girls—Polly, Trixie, and Carol—are like Barney in that they find ways to encourage others to underwrite their often frivolous diversions. As long as they can maintain their self-respect and achieve a satisfactory standard of living, they seem happy with their lot. They are seeking money to enhance their material comfort, not to bankroll some pet social cause that will set the capitalist dogs to howling.

Trixie is the jaded temptress, Polly the ingenue. Only Carol has any real idealistic underpinning—and that is largely built on her feeling that people should be judged for what they are, not on the basis of their family pedigrees.

If we concentrate on the primary focus of the screenplay, we see that *Gold Diggers of 1933* is not really about the Depression or social injustice, it is about romance. Like the Hopwood play, the main story line of the film concentrates on the relationships between Brad and Polly and between J. Lawrence and Carol. The Peabody-Trixie match-up is thrown in for comic relief and gives a further dimension that counterbalances the earnestness of Brad and Polly and the "I have to hate you before I can love you" relationship between J. Lawrence and Carol. The Peabody-Trixie liaison is much more practical than the other two. Even though Peabody has obviously fallen heavily for Trixie ("for the first time in my life, true love, real love, with a real woman—") their relationship is based on a trade-off—financial security for Trixie in return for periodic doting attention to Peabody.

Just to make sure that the course of true love has a few ruts in the road to make matters interesting, there is the mistaken identity convention (a theatrical commonplace extending back through Shakespeare to Plautus). J. Lawrence thinks Carol is the woman his younger brother wants to marry. The resultant confusion, of course, complicates his dealing with Carol when he discovers he is falling for her.

It has been noted that the film could actually hold together if the musical scenes were eliminated. It has also been pointed out that the Berkeley numbers are what save the film from being just another routine comedy of manners.

The Berkeley numbers are designed to afford a marked contrast to the everyday realities of Depression life. Berkeley transports his audience into a world intricately designed and tantalizing. His numbers are obvious extensions of routines that had been a commonplace on the vaudeville stage of an earlier generation. He has explained his intent in creating these visual bonbons for this film: "In an era of breadlines, Depression and wars, I tried to help people get away from all the misery . . . to turn their minds to something else. I wanted to make people happy, if only for an hour."[14]

Mervyn LeRoy reinforces this purpose: "In 1933, my instinct was working overtime. I could feel the public was surfeited, temporarily at least, with the films of realism that had flooded the market since I opened the gates with *Little Caesar*. Now, with the Depression coming to an end, I felt they wanted something gayer, splashier, more lavish. I know I had the urge to make that kind of movie. I had my chance with *Gold Diggers of 1933*."[15]

Happiness, then, is demonstrably the ultimate goal of this film— happiness for the characters and happiness, even if it is only a fleeting experience, for whoever sees the film.

14. Tony Thomas and Jim Terry with Busby Berkeley, *The Busby Berkeley Book* (New York: A & W Visual Library, 1973), p. 9.
15. LeRoy, *Mervyn LeRoy*, p. 119.

1. *Props and pulchritude—two of the staples of any Busby Berkeley dance routine—are shown here in the opening number, "We're in the Money."*

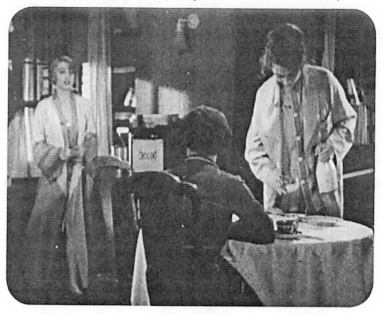

2. *The lot of the unemployed chorus girl. Carol (Joan Blondell), Polly (Ruby Keeler), and Trixie (Aline MacMahon) supplement breakfast in their somewhat tacky flat with a quart of milk pilfered from the fire escape.*

3. *Optimism is reflected in the attractive faces of Polly, Carol, Fay (Ginger Rogers), and Trixie. Barney Hopkins is casting a new show!*

4. *Brad Roberts (Dick Powell), with Rodin's brooding* Thinker *for an audience, shows off his charm and talent as he serenades Polly in the next apartment with one of his own songs.*

5. Barney Hopkins (Ned Sparks) explains that rehearsals for his new show will begin as soon as he gets the money.

6. One of the two main story lines uses the backstage musical convention established in 42nd Street. This shot shows a rehearsal of the "Pettin' in the Park" number.

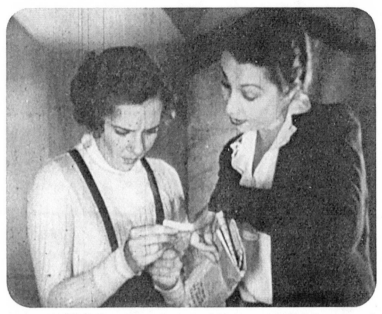

7. A newspaper clipping makes Polly and Trixie suspicious of the source of Brad's money and his real identity.

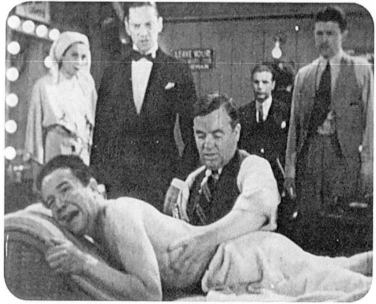

8. Opening night crisis—the "juvenile" lead (Clarence Nordstrom) in Barney's show is felled by an attack of lumbago. Gigolo Eddie's (Tammy Young) ministrations with a gin rubdown fail to relieve the pain.

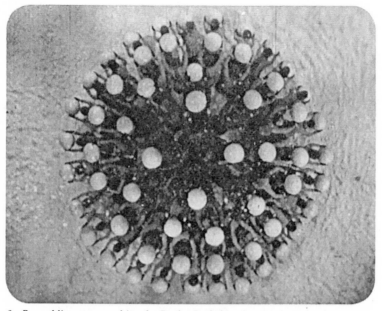

9. *Resembling a sea urchin, the Busby Berkeley chorines hold snowballs over their heads during the winter season segment of "Pettin' in the Park."*

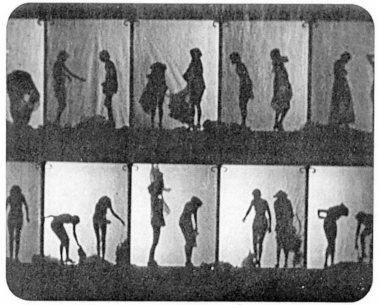

10. *This suggestive tableau occurs during the "Pettin' in the Park" number after a spring shower forces the girls to change clothes behind a translucent, backlighted screen.*

11. *The officious J. Lawrence (Warren William) represents the family in saying that "we cannot have you mixed up in this theater business."*

12. *Peabody (Guy Kibbee) and J. Lawrence, looking as though they both smell something bad, make a voyage of discovery—into the apartment of a trio of chorus girls.*

13. *Trixie, beginning to turn on the gold digger charm, casts an interested glance at Peabody's platinum and gold lighter.*

14. *Carol plays up to J. Lawrence as part of her effort to make him think she is Polly, the girl Brad wants to marry. "Don't be so formal," she says. "You promised to call me—Polly!"*

15. *Peabody compares his face with that of the dog he bought for Trixie.*
"Every time I look at my dog I'll think of you," she said.

16. *J. Lawrence tells Polly that she's not at all cheap and vulgar like people of*
the theater. In high dudgeon, Carol responds for the others: "So we're all too
vulgar for Mr. J. Lawrence Bradford."

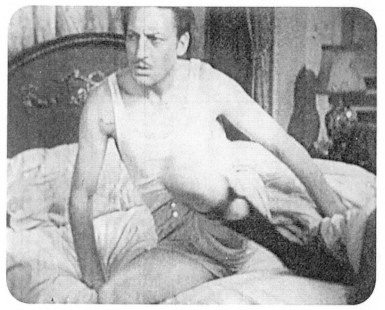

17. *J. Lawrence rises from a strange bed in the girls' apartment after passing out from too much drink the night before.*

18. *J. Lawrence discovers from the paper that Brad has married Polly—and that Carol is not Polly. "I've been tricked," he exclaims. "No doubt about it," Peabody agrees. "They've made a fool of you."*

19. The Berkeley chorines, wearing three-tiered skirts of China silk, dance down an elaborate ramp fashioned for the "Shadow Waltz" number.

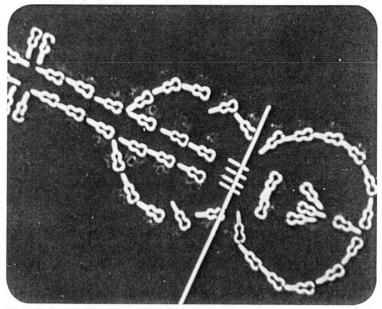

20. In a spectacular sequence from "Shadow Waltz," the chorus—each girl playing a neon-outlined violin—forms a large neon violin.

21. *Though effective cinema, the "Forgotten Man" number has virtually no relationship to the rest of the film.*

22. *Carol sings in the finale as squads of soldiers march in the background and jobless veterans cluster in the foreground.*

Gold Diggers of 1933

Screenplay

by

JAMES SEYMOUR

DAVID BOEHM

and

BEN MARKSON

From the stage play by

AVERY HOPWOOD

Gold Diggers of 1933

FADE IN

1. INT. THEATER   FULL SHOT   STAGE
    Orchestra off playing "We're in the Money." Big happy
    ensemble number, chorus led by Fay, all in costume.
    Carol and Trixie in costume are in front of chorus line.
    Polly dances peppily in first row of chorus. Fay sings cho-
    rus.

2. CLOSE SHOT   FAY
    very cheerful as she sings happy chorus. Chorus in back-
    ground.

> "We're in the Money"
> (Chorus)
> We're in the money
> We're in the money
> We've got a lot of what it takes
>   to get along
> We're in the money
> The skies are sunny
> Old man depression, you are thru,
>   you done us wrong
> We never see a headline
> 'Bout a bread-line today
> And when we see the landlord
> We can look that guy
> Right in the eye
> We're in the money
> Come on my honey
> Let's spend it, lend it,
> Cause we're in the money now!

3.   FLASH   CLOSE SHOT   CAROL AND TRIXIE
smiling, as Fay sings.

QUICK CUT TO:

4.   PAN SHOT   ALONG ROW OF CHORUS GIRLS
as Fay sings. Camera holds when it reaches Polly, full of
life.

QUICK CUT TO:

5.   STAGE   FULL SHOT
as Fay finishes singing chorus and ensemble goes into big
production number—silver coins, etc.[1] Near end of number

TRUCK BACK TO:

6.   STAGE AND AUDITORIUM   FULL SHOT
showing orchestra in shirt-sleeves; empty auditorium
seats; Barney Hopkins, producer, with stage manager and
dance director, standing at rail of orchestra pit, watching
full dress rehearsal. Scattered in auditorium are several
persons, some in costume, watching.

7.   EXT. STAGE DOOR ALLEY   DAY
Music of number heard distantly off. Group of about a
dozen hard-looking workmen, led by sour sheriff, in
derby, descend from parked empty trucks, advance omi-
nously to stage door and enter.

8.   INT. BACKSTAGE NEAR CONCRETE STAIRCASE
which ostensibly leads down to dressing rooms. Gigolo
Eddie, carrying a violin case, stops suddenly as he sees
the sheriff and the latter's men enter the stage door. Gigolo Eddie leans nonchalantly against the guard rail of
the stairway and surreptitiously drops the case down the
steps behind him. There is a crash as the violin case hits
the cement landing.

SHERIFF (looking around):
    What was that?

Eddie innocently shrugs his shoulders.[2]

CUT TO:

9.   CLOSE SHOT ON THE STAIRWAY LANDING
The violin case has burst open. Instead of a violin it has been filled with bottles of whiskey, all of which are smashed.

10.   INT. BACKSTAGE
Music of number loud off. Sheriff and men, very businesslike, walk up behind big flat or set piece of scenery. They pause, looking up at it.

SHERIFF (gruffly):
    Might as well begin here, boys!

Men lay hold of scenery.

11.   STAGE   FULL SHOT
Ensemble doing number. Behind them scenery suddenly begins to move off stage, without visible means of locomotion. Members of ensemble nearest scenery stop dancing, surprised, watch scenery moved off. One by one others pause in amazement as scenery near them moves away. Workmen are now visible dismantling set.

12.   STAGE AND AUDITORIUM   FULL SHOT
as several members of orchestra stop playing. Barney protests in frenzy.

BARNEY (shouting):
    Hey! What's the idea?

Everyone has now stopped singing and dancing except Polly, who dances alone center stage. As Barney starts to scramble angrily up onto stage, Polly suddenly realizes situation and stops also. Everyone stares as scenery is carried out.

13.   STAGE   FULL SHOT
Barney angrily faces boss sheriff.

BARNEY:
What is this? What is this?

SHERIFF:
Who are you?

BARNEY:
I'm Barney Hopkins—producer of this show!

SHERIFF:
Tough luck, brother. I'm from the sheriff's office. Legal attachment to pay creditors. Corpus delicti—or seize the body!

A workman grabs arm of Fay, who has slumped into chair.

FAY (shrieking):
Don't you dare!

WORKMAN:
Sorry to disappoint you, sister.

He takes chair away, doing nothing to her.

14.   CLOSE SHOT   GIGOLO EDDIE
as he overhears the sheriff's words. He looks ruefully down toward the broken bottles, then turns to stage manager who is standing near him.

GIGOLO EDDIE (to stage manager):
Can you imagine that. I thought he was after me. (Points down to broken bottles.) There goes this week's profits.

15.   STAGE   FULL SHOT
Protesting Barney follows sheriff, who pays no attention to him.

BARNEY:
Now, listen! We got a show. Tomorrow night we open. You can't do this to me—just because I don't

pay a few bills! When the show opens, I'll pay them.

Workmen continue removing stuff, ignoring members of company. Everyone complains, beefing loudly about attachment and stopping of show, ad lib.

POLLY (amazed):
What's the excitement?

GIRL:
They're attaching us.

POLLY:
What does that mean?

GIRL:
I don't know. It's something like a raid, I guess.

FAY (sore):
It means they stop the show, dumbbell.

CAROL:
This is the fourth in two months I've been in of and out of.

TRIXIE:
They close before they open!

CHORUS MAN:
It's the Depression, dearie.

DISSOLVE TO:

16.   FLASH   EXT. THEATER
closed.

QUICK CUT TO:

17.   FLASH   EXT. ANOTHER THEATER
dark.

QUICK CUT TO:

18.   FLASH   EXT. THIRD THEATER
Big sign: Closed until Further Notice.

QUICK DISSOLVE TO:

19.   FLASH   INT. TICKET AGENCY   FULL SHOT
Sign: Bryson's Theater Tickets. Not a customer at counter, where yawning clerk leans with nothing to do. Behind counter on wall, bulletin board of current attractions shows word Closed next to almost every theater name.

QUICK DISSOLVE TO:

20.   FLASH   INT. BOOKING OFFICE   FULL SHOT
Empty, except for drowsing secretary. Sign on wall: Star Theatrical Agency; under it crude sign: No Jobs Available.

DISSOLVE TO:

21.   INT. BEDROOM   FULL SHOT   TWIN BEDS AND COUCH
In the twin beds are Trixie and Carol. Polly is on the couch. Three pairs of eyes open wearily. Three heads turn and gaze at silent alarm clock on stand by bed.

TRIXIE:

I can remember when that alarm clock used to ring. Those good old days when we *had* to get up.

CAROL:

What a memory! Didn't there used to be something called a job—or am I wrong again?

POLLY:

You're right for once. Let's get up and look for work. I hate starving in bed.

TRIXIE:

Name a better place to starve.

CAROL (dryly):

In your stomach. (Alternate line.) At a banquet.

Trixie heaves herself out of bed, starts putting on slippers and kimono. Polly sits up in bed.

TRIXIE:

It's all right to kid about it, but just the same it's the bunk. All people want is a chance to work—and they can't.

CAROL (stretching her arms as she lies back on pillow):
I almost got a job yesterday running an elevator.

Trixie stands regarding Carol, shaking her head.

TRIXIE (ironically):
Carol King, torch singer, the burnt toast of Broadway, running an elevator! The world is certainly cockeyed!

CAROL (bitterly):
There were two hundred in line ahead of me . . . (smiles suddenly) thank heaven!

POLLY (scrambling out of bed):
Fay is working in Starr's Drugstore. She's trying to get me a job there. They're only paying seven a week and no tips any more, but you get your meals.

TRIXIE:
Well, let's get dressed. We'll try the flea circus this morning. Maybe there's something for us there.

POLLY:
What can we get at the flea circus?

TRIXIE (with a look):
Fleas!

Carol throws a shoe at her.[3]

DISSOLVE TO:

22.   INT. BEDROOM   FULL SHOT
The three girls, partially dressed, are putting on their stockings. Polly stops, a hole in hers.

POLLY:
My *last*!

CAROL:
Here's another pair. I was saving these but—

Carol throws Polly another pair.

53

POLLY (reluctantly):
I can go barelegged.

TRIXIE:
In this weather? And get pneumonia? Who's going to pay for the doctor?

Polly nods ruefully and draws on stockings, then rises, stops near window, and starts going through setting-up and limbering exercises.

TRIXIE:
Cut that out. Do you want to work up an appetite when we're so broke?

CAROL:
She's only taking bows. Ring for an audience.

POLLY (as she continues):
I've got to keep in trim.

TRIXIE:
For what? There's only two things to keep in trim for—shows—and there are no shows—men—and there are no— Oh, I forgot, *you're in love*.

CAROL (to Trixie, coming to Polly's defense):
What's wrong with that? I'll bet you wish you were, too.

TRIXIE:
Oh, I wish I was, do I? Even love is not what it used to be. When show business was slow, I used to live on my alimony. Now I can't collect a cent of it. Married three of them against a rainy day. Now it's pouring and they haven't an umbrella between them!

Polly has finished exercising, and the three girls, now dressed, start out of the room.

22A.   LIVING ROOM   FULL SHOT
as three girls enter from bedroom.

CAROL:
How about a little nourishment?

She crosses to kitchenette as Polly gets dishes and cutlery from drawer.

POLLY:
What's on the menu?

Trixie crosses to hall door, purposefully.

TRIXIE (hand on knob):
I'll see what the neighbors have to offer!

23.   FULL SHOT   APARTMENT HOUSE HALLWAY
as Trixie opens door cautiously, peers up and down the hall and tiptoes to door of next apartment, picks up bottle of milk beside it, and scuttles back into her own apartment.[4]

24.   INT. LIVING ROOM   FULL SHOT   ANGLING TOWARD SMALL KITCHENETTE SEPARATED FROM LIVING ROOM BY CURTAINS
as Trixie reenters triumphantly carrying a bottle of milk. Carol at kitchenette slicing bread. Polly setting table.

CAROL (as she makes toast):
I can remember not so long ago, a penthouse on Park Avenue, with a real tree, and flowers, and a fountain, and a French maid, and a warm bath perfumed with salts from Yardley, and a dress, a little model of Schiaparelli's, and downstairs a snappy roadster, and a drive through the park—and now—stealing milk!

TRIXIE (grimly):
That's all right. The dairy company stole it from a cow . . . (Then sentimentally.) Just a year ago I was on my way to Havana—and birds were singing— and the skies were blue—and I said to the big mug in the next pew—"I need a couple of hundred dollars, Big Boy"—and he said, "In my pants pocket"— and I just reached over and took five hundred dollars

out of his pants pocket—just like that— (Sighs.) And
now I have to go out and kidnap a bottle of milk!

25.   INT. LIVING ROOM   FULL SHOT
        ANGLING TOWARD KITCHENETTE TAKING IN PIANO
Trixie has gotten glasses and proceeded to pour out milk.
There is a sudden knock at the door. All pause, startled
and apprehensive. Shaking her head sadly, Trixie starts to
pour milk back into bottle.

TRIXIE:
    Well, guess we have to give it back.

Carol puts down plate of toast on table and turns ruefully
toward piano.

CAROL:
    It's probably about the piano. (Patting keys.) Good-
    bye, old thing. Don't forget to brush your teeth.

Polly crosses after another knock comes at the door and
opens it, admitting a girl wearing big dark glasses, her
coat collar turned up. The three girls regard her, surprised.

TRIXIE:
    Oh, it's you.

POLLY:
    Fay!

FAY (removing glasses and turning down collar):
    In the flesh. A hundred and eight pounds of charm-
    ing young womanhood.

CAROL:
    Why the blue spectacles, grandma?

FAY:
    So the landlady wouldn't recognize me . . . You know
    I'm obligated to her for a little item called rent.

TRIXIE (suspiciously):
If you've come to make a touch, the bank has folded.

FAY:
Your millions are safe, Trixie. I came to tell you girls news. Barney is putting on a new show.

POLLY (greatly excited):
Barney?

CAROL:
Barney Hopkins?

FAY:
Rehearsals start in two weeks.

CAROL:
Barney must have dug up an angel.

POLLY:
Let's go over and find out.

CAROL:
That's right. Soon as it gets around, there'll be a mob after him.

POLLY:
Let's hurry.

TRIXIE:
We can't all go. There's hardly enough decent clothing left to wrap around one of us.

FAY:
If one doesn't look modish with Barney, it's thumbs down.

TRIXIE:
Well, let's see if we can scare up enough for one of us to look—as you say—*modish*. Who's to go?

CAROL:
Let's match for it.

POLLY:
> Taxis!

Four girls hustle to window.

TRIXIE:
> Yellow!

CAROL:
> Checker!

FAY:
> Red Top!

POLLY:
> Black and White!

Girls crane out window, looking down into street.

26. LONG SHOT   DOWN ON STREET
Girls at window in foreground. First taxicab to appear in traffic is Checker.

FOUR GIRLS (in chorus):
> Checker!

They turn excitedly back into room.

27. INT. LIVING ROOM   FULL SHOT

POLLY:
> Carol wins.

FAY:
> I look so much better in clothes than any of you. If Barney saw me in clothes—

TRIXIE:
> He wouldn't recognize you!

Trixie helps Carol out of her dress.

FAY (to Trixie):
> Where's your lovely mink coat?

TRIXIE:
Uncle has it. Uncle has everything. We've even hocked our inlays.

POLLY:
You'll look adorable in this hat.

Polly tries hat on Carol, who is now in underthings, and holds bag Trixie gave her.

CAROL:
Darling, I'll have to take those stockings back.

POLLY:
Oh, sure.

Polly takes off stockings. Meanwhile, Trixie attacks Fay and takes off her dress.

FAY:
Don't. I have to go back to the drugstore.

TRIXIE:
We'll give you something good enough for a drugstore.

FAY:
But the dress belongs to them. I'm a hostess.

CAROL:
So am I a hostess. I'm going to entertain Barney with the idea of putting us to work!

TRIXIE (putting dress on Carol):
Stand in the light, honey, when you talk to Barney. They know what they're doing when they dress their hostesses at *that* drugstore.

DISSOLVE TO:

28.   FULL SHOT
Carol, now fully dressed, and Fay, in borrowed dress, are about to start out together, with Trixie and Polly wishing Carol luck. Trixie takes a couple of dollar bills from her purse.

TRIXIE (handing bills to Carol):
Here, kid, take these papers, get through the enemy's
lines, and ride like blazes . . . Taxi fare.

POLLY:
Lots of luck, Carol.

FAY (to Carol as they start out; meaningfully):
Watch yourself in the clinches. Remember that's my
dress.

The door closes after them.

TRIXIE (bitterly):
And now, the best comedienne on Broadway will
proceed to make beds.

Polly laughs and begins to gather up dishes. Suddenly
comes sound of piano and Brad's voice from other apartment across court. Polly's face lights up. She crosses happily toward window and leans out. CAMERA ZOOMS past
her out window to:

29.   WINDOW OPPOSITE   FULL SHOT
Just inside open window, Brad Roberts, at piano, plays
and sings "Shadow Waltz." Polly's voice, off, joins in,
singing with him. Brad looks up out window, smiles
across at Polly, waves as he finishes verse.

"Shadow Waltz"
(Chorus)
In the shadow let me
Come and sing to you
Let me dream a song that
I can bring to you
Take me in your arms and
Let me cling to you
Let me linger long,
Let me live my song.
In the winter let me
Bring the spring to you

Let me feel that I
>   Mean ev'rything to you
>   Love's old song—will be new
>   In the shadow
>   When I come and sing to you.

30.   FULL SHOT   POLLY AT WINDOW   FROM BRAD'S ANGLE
as Brad, off, finishes playing verse and starts chorus. Polly smiles, waves, and continues singing chorus.

31.   EXT. FULL SHOT   BOTH WINDOWS
as Brad starts singing chorus with Polly. Together they sing chorus happily through to end.

32.   INT. LIVING ROOM
Trixie enters from bedroom carrying bundle of dirty sheets and pillowcases as Polly throws kiss to Brad.

TRIXIE (sardonically):
>   I can't turn *these* sheets anymore. They've only got two sides!

Polly starts, turns in from window, flustered. Trixie catches on.

TRIXIE:
>   Un-huh! Mooning over that good-for-nothing songwriter again! Where's that going to get you?

POLLY:
>   He's *wonderful!*

TRIXIE (as if ending all discussion):
>   Honey, he's a *songwriter*.

POLLY:
>   So is Irving Berlin. What's wrong about a songwriter?

61

TRIXIE:

>   Don't ask me . . . How long have you known that
>   boy? Two weeks. What do you know about him?

POLLY:

>   I knew everything I wanted to know the minute I
>   met him.

Telephone rings. Trixie and Polly start eagerly. Polly rushes
to phone.

POLLY:

>   Hello . . . ? (To Trixie.) It's Carol!

Trixie joins her excitedly, as Polly listens eagerly.

33.   CLOSE SHOT   CAROL   IN PHONE BOOTH
Tears of happiness in her eyes, nodding excitedly into
phone.

CAROL:

>   It's true! Really true! He's putting on the show!

34.   INT. LIVING ROOM
Polly at phone turns, thrilled, to waiting Trixie.

POLLY:

>   It's true. Barney's putting on the show!

Polly returns to phone.

35.   CLOSE SHOT   CAROL AT PHONE

CAROL:

>   I'm bringing him up to the apartment! Be there in
>   ten minutes . . . Phone the other girls—phone
>   everybody . . . Tell them to get ready! He hasn't cast
>   yet!

36.   INT. LIVING ROOM
Polly nods, enthusiastically.

POLLY (in phone):
> All right—I will . . . Hurry . . . and don't lose him!
> (Hangs up, turns to Trixie.) They're coming up!

TRIXIE:
> Who?

POLLY:
> Barney and Carol. Phone Fay! Phone the girls . . .
> We're all set.

TRIXIE:
> You phone . . . I've got to dig up the last of the old
> sex appeal! And the way I feel I'll probably have to
> use a steam shovel!

Trixie hurries into bedroom as Polly consults book of
phone numbers and starts to dial.
NOTE: Following series of quick dissolves should have
bright, amusing musical background.

37. INT. TELEPHONE EXCHANGE   FULL SHOT
Girls before switchboard, all very busy, babble of voices.

38. CLOSE SHOT   PRETTY BLONDE OPERATOR
as she listens. She nods, happily excited. With sweep of
hand she removes all wires from board, which begins immediately to flash frantic signals. Girl removes earphones,
slams them down, rises, looks down at switchboard with
great disdain, waves it a mocking good-bye, and beats it.
WIPE OFF TO:

39. INT. PRIVATE OFFICE   CLOSE SHOT   BOSS AND SECRETARY
He sits at desk; overrouged, underdressed, luscious bru-
nette secretary on his lap. His eyes are popping, his
hands busy, the secretary submissive. Phone rings. Girl
disentangles herself.

40. FULL SHOT   AT DESK
Secretary answers phone.

SECRETARY (into phone):
Yes . . . ? What . . . ? *What* . . . ! Yes . . . !

She hangs up, faces boss, adjusts blouse, loosens belt so charms are less obvious, pulls down skirt, removes some rouge and mascara.

BOSS (puzzled):
What's the trouble, sweetheart?

SECRETARY:
I'm through with this racket . . . I'm going back to the legit . . . Eight shows a week—and no benefit performances for the boss.

With a toss of head, she walks out on stunned boss.

WIPE OFF TO:

41.   INT. ART SCHOOL   FULL SHOT
Life class of students working. On dais in background, nude model partially hidden by drawing boards and canvases. Sign on wall reads Ruben's Art School. Female clerk enters, advances between students, and whispers to model. Model grins, lets out whoop, wraps robe around her, leaps down off dais, and beats it, tipping over easels, etc., in confusion of her rush.

WIPE OFF TO:

42.   EXT. STORE WINDOW   FULL SHOT   DAY
People watching lovely girl demonstrating—with very bored air—"unbreakable" glassware. Girl in foreground outside window, attracts demonstrator's attention, scribbles note with her lipstick on envelope, and holds it up against windowpane for demonstrator to read.

INSERT   CLOSE-UP   NOTE AGAINST GLASS
CRUDELY PRINTED
"Barney putting on show—meet me out front! "

BACK TO SCENE:
Demonstrator reads, nods happily, deliberately picks up

and smashes a lot of the "unbreakable" glassware, and ducks off window platform.

WIPE OFF TO:

43.   INT. SICK ROOM   FULL SHOT   PATIENT IN BED
eyes closed. Pretty nurse enters, thermometer in hand, scowls at patient. Patient opens eyes, nurse puts on sweet smile, and sticks thermometer in mouth. Phone tinkles gently. Nurse answers it, listens nodding and smiling, hangs up. She does pirouette by bed.

NURSE (shout of delight):
    Yippee!

Patient watches her amazed. Nurse tears off apron and cap, chucks them at patient's head, and rushes off. Patient sits bolt upright, head sticking up through apron, cap over an ear, and thermometer tilting ludicrously from mouth as he stares after nurse.

WIPE OFF TO:

44.   INT. GIRL'S ROOM   FULL SHOT   GIRL AND MAN ON COUCH
in close embrace.

MAN (passionately);
    I'll gladly marry you—Tuesday—

Girl draws back momentarily, then sighs and gives in. As man grabs her, the phone rings. Girl reaches over, man's arms still about her, picks up French phone.

GIRL:
    Hello . . . ? Yes . . .

Her face lights up. She hangs up, frees herself, rises calmly, and puts on her hat. Man rises surprised. Girl turns to him, smiling pleasantly, then quite matter-of-fact slaps his face hard, and walks out without a word.[5]

Musical background fades as we

DISSOLVE TO:

45. LIVING ROOM   FULL SHOT
Trixie, now all dolled up to receive producer, hustles
about, tidying up room, arranging pillows, etc.

TRIXIE (calling off toward bedroom):
Step on it, Polly—they ought to be here any minute.

POLLY'S VOICE OFF:
Almost ready!

Trixie opens door, sticks head out, peeking up and down
hall. As she returns, Polly enters from bedroom looking
very cute. Trixie makes her turn around, nods approv-
ingly.

POLLY:
Gosh, to think we might have jobs again—earn
money—

TRIXIE:
Yeah, and I've been off the gold standard *so* long—

Sharp tattoo at door.

POLLY (breathlessly):
It's them!

Trixie and Polly primp, nervously thrilled, fixing themselves with last moment dabs. Polly opens door, revealing
Carol, all smiles, and the dour Barney.

CAROL:
Come on in, Barney, meet the girls.

POLLY:
Hello, Mr. Hopkins.

BARNEY:
Hello!

Trixie, standing in light of window, poses a moment.
Barney seems not to notice, sits down gloomy faced.
Trixie's face falls, but she sweeps effusively over to Bar-
ney, making much of him.

66

TRIXIE:

Well, Barney! Good old smiling, big-hearted Barney. I hear you're doing a show.

BARNEY:

Yes, I'm doing a show.

TRIXIE:

You're more enthusiastic than usual. Does that mean it's good?

BARNEY:

You said it's good. It's the finest thing I've ever had . . .

The three girls are hovering about Barney, hanging on his every word, trying to make him extra comfortable. A knock at door. Carol admits one of the girls we saw quit her job. Carol motions her to silence, in pantomime indicates Barney, and girl sits down quietly as Barney continues.

BARNEY (continuing):

I've figured it from every angle and I don't see how it can run less than six months or gross less than half a million . . . That's figuring on thirty grand a week, and at the Broadhurst, we can do forty . . . We'll do forty with this show.

POLLY (awed):

Gosh!

BARNEY (noticing Polly):

I remember you.

POLLY:

Do you?

BARNEY:

You were in the chorus. You're coming out of the chorus some day. You've got stuff on the ball.

POLLY (thrilled):
Oh, thank you, Mr. Hopkins.

GIRL (piping up from her place):
Can you use me, too, Mr. Hopkins?

BARNEY (in a big way):
I'll use all you girls I used before. (All murmur delightedly.) Carol here will be featured—and Trixie, as comic . . . Got some ideas for song numbers for you, Carol, that will tear their hearts out. Something new—*different!*

Brad on his piano across the court starts playing "I've Got to Sing a Torch Song." Engrossed, no one notices.

TRIXIE:
What's the show about?

BARNEY:
The show is about the Depression. My idea is—

Barney pauses, listening, as he suddenly notices Brad's music. He shows interest.

BARNEY:
Who's that playing?

TRIXIE:
A palooka—songwriter!

Barney rises, crosses to window. Polly, showing her delight, goes with him.

BARNEY:
I've never heard that number. What is it?

POLLY (proudly):
It's his own. He composes music.

TRIXIE (irritated at interruption):
Shut the window and let's get on with this.

She starts for window.

BARNEY:
  Wait . . . That's not bad . . . Tell the fellow to come on over.

POLLY (quickly calling out window):
  Brad!

BRAD'S VOICE OFF:
  What?

POLLY (out window):
  Come on over—quick!

BARNEY (serious):
  That tune has a great feel to it—the boy's got something.

TRIXIE (sour):
  Yeah—ambition.

BARNEY:
  What's he done?

Trixie shrugs, about to say something derogatory. Polly hastily interrupts.

POLLY (to Barney):
  He hasn't had a chance to do anything, *yet*, but he has genius. Really, Mr. Hopkins.

BARNEY:
  We can use a little genius in the show business.

Knock at door. Polly flies to open it. Trixie is disturbed, speaks as Polly admits Brad.

TRIXIE (to Barney):
  What's the idea, taking up time with a genius when there are hard-working girls like us to worry about?

BRAD (to Polly):
  What is it?

Polly excitedly drags Brad over to Barney.

POLLY:
This is Brad Roberts, Mr. Hopkins.

BARNEY (nods abruptly):
Sit down and play.

BRAD:
Play what?

BARNEY:
That number you were just playing.

Carol and Polly urge Brad to piano.

CAROL (to Brad):
Go ahead—don't be afraid. You're among friends!

Brad sits, plays and sings chorus of "I've Got to Sing a Torch Song."

"I've Got to Sing a Torch Song"
(Chorus)
I've got to sing a torch song
For that's the way I feel
When I feel a thing, then I can sing,
It must be real
I couldn't sing a gay song
It wouldn't be sincere
I could never croon a happy tune
Without a tear
I have my dreams but one by one
They vanish in the sky,
I try to smile and face the sun
But romance passes by, that's why
I've got to sing a torch song
To someone far apart
For the torch I bear is burning there
Right in my heart.

Barney listens with growing approval. As Brad finishes, Barney rises enthusiastically, claps Brad on back.

BARNEY:
> Swell—I like it. Got anything else?

BRAD:
> Yes—a couple of things.

BARNEY:
> Let's hear them—

Brad returns to piano, starts to play. Barney paces room listening. Knock at door. Barney glares, opens door, and admits Fay, who smiles a greeting as Brad plays.

FAY (very coy):
> Hello, Mr. Hopkins. Charming to see you again!

BARNEY (gruffly, gesturing her to sit down):
> Sit down—sit down!

Fay subsides quietly, in chair. Barney resumes pacing, then interrupts Brad.

BARNEY (to Brad):
> No—I don't like that. It's dull.

Brad stops playing. Trixie tries to bring conversation back to the really important matter of jobs for the girls.

TRIXIE:
> What is this? A piano lesson? Or are we going to hear about this show?

Barney silences her with a gesture, intent on his musical comedy idea.

BARNEY (to Brad):
> You haven't something—with a sort of march effect—march rhythm to it?

BRAD (nods eagerly):
> Yes, I have . . . Yes . . . "Remember My Forgotten Man."

Brad starts to play as he talks.

BRAD (continuing as he plays):
I haven't any words to this yet—I tell you, I just got the idea for it last night—watching the men on that bread line on Times Square—in the rain, standing waiting for doughnuts and coffee—men out of a job . . . the soup kitchen—

BARNEY (himself excited as Brad plays):
Stop . . . Go on . . . Wait . . . That's just what this show's about—the Depression—men marching—marching in the rain—marching—marching—doughnuts and crullers—jobs—jobs—marching—marching—marching in the rain—and in the background will be Carol—spirit of the Depression—a blue song—no, not a blue song—but a wailing—a wailing—and this woman—this gorgeous woman—singing this number that tears your heart out—the big parade—the big parade of tears—

Brad, nodding his understanding, as he plays. Barney yells enthusiastically at him.

BARNEY:
Yeah—yeah—that's it! Work on it. Work on it.

Another knock at door and two girls enter. Barney sees them, nods and bellows at them as he points.

BARNEY:
You, too—I'm going to use you! All of you!

FAY (rising):
I'd like to do a specialty.

BARNEY (impatiently):
Sit down or you'll do a blockout! (Back to Brad as he finishes playing.) I'll cancel my contract with Warren and Dubin! They're out! *You're* going to write the *music* for me—and lyrics! Can you write lyrics?

POLLY:

> You bet he can.

Another girl enters. Barney frowns at her.

BARNEY:

> What's happened to you? What's your name—No-
> rah—you got thin. You're just skin and bones.

NORAH:

> Been tough going. I'll fatten up.

BARNEY:

> No, don't fatten up. I'm going to take some of you
> skinny ones and use you—show them—what this
> Depression is—what a messy thing it is—make a
> great number—I got it all figured out—(He turns
> quickly to Brad.) I want your stuff, son. It's good. I
> *definitely* want it.

BRAD:

> Mr. Hopkins, you can have it—on one condition.

BARNEY (suspicious):
> Yeah?

BRAD:

> If Miss Parker, Polly, has a principal part in the show.
> She's helped me a lot—and she's *really* great!

BARNEY:

> You telling me? I'm telling you. I'll tell you some-
> thing else. You've got a swell voice, too . . . and per-
> sonality. You're different—you've got class. I want
> you to sing in this show.

BRAD (startled):

> No, not me. No, that's impossible . . . You can have
> my music, but—

BARNEY:

> You and Polly would make a smart team—like the
> Astaires.[6] You'd be a knockout for the *mush* interest.

73

BRAD (serious):
No, that's quite impossible. I won't even discuss it.

POLLY:
But Brad, why not?

BRAD:
I can't, honey. For a lot of reasons—

TRIXIE (interrupting):
Hey, let me get on for a minute! Isn't there any comedy in this show?

BARNEY:
Plenty . . . The gay side, the hard-boiled side, the cynical and funny side of the Depression . . . I'll make 'em laugh at you starving to death! Be the best thing you ever did, Trixie.

TRIXIE:
Yeah! Have you ever seen me ride a horse?

CAROL (businesslike):
When do rehearsals begin, Barney?

BARNEY:
Rehearsals? (His face falls, he shrugs ruefully.) They begin as soon as I get the money.

TRIXIE:
Get the money!

GENERAL SHOUT:
What! No money?

BARNEY:
That's always the way it is. I got the show, I got the music, I got the theater, I got the cast—everybody raring to go—and it's the old, old story. Money!

CAROL:
No money at all?

BARNEY:

Not even the old shoestring.

CAROL:

But Barney, you said—you made us think—

BARNEY:

What did I make you think? I said I had a show—a great show—and I have!

FAY (indignant):
You said it was *set*.

BARNEY:

It is set. Been set for six months. Every time I get an angel to put up the money, something happens . . . Just today I had someone, just today he comes to me and says he and his wife who was suing him for a divorce—they've been reconciled—and she don't want him fooling around with the show business. And there I am, holding the bag—

He drops into chair, disgusted. Everyone else is dumb, thunderstruck. Carol shakes a stern finger at Barney.

CAROL:

You've got a lot of nerve, Barney. What about all these girls? They've thrown up jobs—just because you said— You ought to be ashamed of yourself, Barney— Isn't it tough enough without you making mugs out of us? We counted on this— Every one of us—

Barney rises looking about room at the glum faces, tries to placate them.

BARNEY:

Listen—Listen, kids—I'm not going to let you down. I got other irons in the fire. Don't worry. Couple of men coming from out of town. Due here tomorrow— Texas— Cattle—

Barney moves about room, but gets no cheerful reactions.

TRIXIE:
> Yeah, Texas— Cattle—How can they sell cattle? Who eats meat anymore?

BARNEY:
> All I can say is—

Barney finds nothing to say, makes an expressive gesture of helplessness. There is a pause—dead dreary silence. Brad, who has watched quietly from piano, speaks.

BRAD (casually):
> How much do you need?

BARNEY (hopelessly):
> Say—fifty thousand dollars.

CAROL:
> Stop kidding, Barney. There isn't fifty thousand dollars in the world. Not to put a show on, anyway.

BARNEY:
> All right. Who needs fifty thousand? Forty . . . twenty-five. (Carol shakes her head.) If I chisel—and I know how to chisel—I could do it for fifteen . . . Yeah, it would be a cinch—fifteen—*but*—

BRAD (calmly as he rises):
> I'll advance you fifteen.

BARNEY (in amazement):
> What?

Everyone starts in surprise. Trixie stares at Brad, shaking her head sympathetically.

TRIXIE:
> Say, what does he use? I'll smoke it, too. (To Brad.) Quit joking, will you? It's not smart to make gags when girls are starving.

POLLY (seriously):
> It's too serious a matter to all of us, Brad.

Polly puts her hand on Brad's arm. Brad takes out check-book. Everyone stares, unable to believe their eyes and ears.

BRAD (writing check):
I'm not wisecracking. I'll be glad to do it.

CAROL:
Where can *you* get fifteen grand from? He means real money—not streetcar transfers.

BRAD (pauses in writing check; to Barney):
Remember, one condition—Polly is featured.

BARNEY (hastily):
Anything you say—her name in lights—anything.

Brad resumes writing check, then hesitates. All watch with baited breath. Brad frowns to himself, then rips check out of book and tears it up. Everyone winces, relaxing again into despair.

BRAD (seriously):
No, I can't give you a check—for certain reasons . . . (Barney sighs hopelessly.) I'll give you cash to-morrow. Is that all right?

Barney stands speechless. It looks like a gag. All the girls try to pretend they knew all along that Brad was joking, but their laughter is forced.

TRIXIE (trying to laugh it off):
And you fell for it, Barney!

FAY:
He did . . . ! He fell for it . . . ! It's what is commonly known as a gag.

BRAD (sincerely):
It's not a gag. I mean it.

POLLY (hurt at Brad's apparent joke on them):
Oh, Brad.

Brad looks around puzzled.

BRAD (to Barney):
Tomorrow—cash—I'll be at your office at ten-thirty—
You have my word for it . . . (Then in growing ex-
citement.) Say, I've got another idea—for a number—
I'll see you later.

Brad hurries out. Everyone is silent. Polly follows him.

46.   INT. HALL   FULL SHOT
Brad going down hall. Polly comes from apartment,
calls.

POLLY:
Brad— (He pauses, she overtakes him) this is cruel.

BRAD:
What?

POLLY:
To kid about a thing like this—

BRAD:
I'm not kidding. I'll give him the money. He'll have
it in his office at half past ten tomorrow morning.

POLLY:
Where are you going to get fifteen thousand dollars?

Brad starts to say something, pauses, then tries to cover
up his hesitation.

BRAD (lightly):
See this ring? I just turn it and make a wish—and—

POLLY (hurt at his jesting):
Brad!

BRAD (pleading):
Trust me, honey—and I'm *not* joking.

POLLY:
That's just the trouble. *I* do trust you.

BRAD:

> Honey— (He breaks off, wanting to tell her he loves her.)

POLLY:

> What?

BRAD (thinking better of it):

> I won't say it yet . . . I have an idea . . . I want to get to the piano before I lose it. (He turns away hurriedly.) I'll see you later.

Polly watches him go, then turns back to apartment.

47.   INT. LIVING ROOM   FULL SHOT

All are sitting and standing about in despair. Barney leans head in hands. Polly reenters.

POLLY:

> He meant it. Really he did . . . I'll stake my life on it.

Barney does not even look up.

TRIXIE:

> Faith, hope, and charity. You have faith, Barney has hopes, and we all need charity.

From outside comes sound of Brad playing "I've Got to Sing a Torch Song." Barney raises his head as he hears it.

BARNEY:

> Shut up a minute . . . Listen . . . ! He's got it. Got just what I want . . . Hear that wailing . . . Gee, don't that just get you?

All listen, moved by the music. Carol lights a cigarette and drifts over to the window. She leans there listening, then begins to hum, softly at first, then sings full.

                              FADE OUT

FADE IN

INSERT   CLOSE-UP   CLOCK

marking eleven o'clock.

48.   FLASH   CLOSE-UP   CAROL'S HAND
on desk fingers tapping nervously.

49.   FLASH   CLOSE-UP   POLLY'S TWO HANDS
in her lap, anxiously twisting handkerchief.

50.   FLASH   CLOSE-UP   BARNEY'S FEET
pacing excitedly.

51.   FLASH   CLOSE-UP   TRIXIE'S FOOT
tapping impatiently.

INSERT   FLASH   CLOSE-UP   BARNEY'S WATCH
marking twelve o'clock.

52.   INT. BARNEY'S OFFICE   FULL SHOT   DAY
Barney shakes head despairingly, stuffs watch back in
pocket, and begins pacing. Trixie stands watching exas-
peratedly, starts pacing, too, belligerently. Polly sits, dis-
consolately, on verge of tears. Carol, by desk, watches
Polly sympathetically. Secretary is listening at phone,
hangs up, and turns to Barney, shaking her head.

SECRETARY:
No answer at his apartment.

Carol sits beside Polly, puts her arm around shoulder
comfortingly. Barney sits down at desk, licked. Trixie sits
down stiffly, glaring at Barney.

TRIXIE:
And now Trixie can say, "I told you so," only I *won't*—
it hurts too much.

There is a knock at the door. Everyone present sits up
expectantly.

BARNEY (heartily):
Come in! Come in!

The door opens and Gigolo Eddie comes in, carrying a
brief case. All present sit back in disappointment.

BARNEY (sitting down dejectedly):
Oh, it's you.

TRIXIE:
Gigolo Eddie—always shows up at the wrong time.

GIGOLO EDDIE (opening his briefcase and taking out a bottle):
Heard you got your mitts on some dough to open the show. Thought you might want to celebrate. (Holds up the bottle.) Fresh from the boat.

BARNEY:
You heard wrong, Eddie. Pull up a coffin and lie down with the rest of us.

Eddie sits down.

GIGOLO EDDIE:
Business is sure tough. Nobody even wants to owe me any more.

BARNEY (to secretary):
You can go.

SECRETARY:
You hired me for the day.

BARNEY:
I thought I might need a secretary.

SECRETARY:
You'll pay me for the day, or I'll complain to the agency!

She rises and exits.

BARNEY:
I wish I had somebody to complain to . . .

There is a sudden knock at door. Everyone revives again eagerly, except Barney, who frowns skeptically. Polly leaps to door and opens it. In file four dapper young Broadway types (suggestion of Jewishness). They are all dressed ex-

actly alike, immaculate in morning coats, spats, black der-
bies, gloves. Each carries mandolin case. They stand side
by side facing Barney.

BARNEY (puzzled):
    Well–who are you?

FIRST MAN (in broad Hebe dialect):
    Ve're de Kaintucky Heel-Beelies!

Simultaneously the four turn their mandolin cases revealing the printed words, one word on each case:
The Kentucky Hill Billies.

FIRST MAN:
    Songs!

SECOND MAN (Hebe dialect):
    Dences!

THIRD MAN (Hebe dialect):
    Moosic!

FOURTH MAN (Hebe accent):
    Vise crecks! (Wise cracks!)

GIGOLO EDDIE (menacingly):
    Kentucky Hill Billies? Moonshiners! Trying to mus-
    cle in, huh?

BARNEY (disgusted):
    Pipe down, Eddie. (To quartet.) Do you know "Your
    Old Kentucky Home"?

FOUR MEN (enthusiastically, in chorus):
    Sure!

BARNEY (shoving them out door):
    Then scram back there—your old *mammy's* looking
    for you!

He slams door after them and drops into chair dejectedly.

BARNEY (gloomily):
Might as well close up the joint—before the acrobats and midgets start flocking in!

Suddenly the door opens and Brad enters breezily. Barney and the others regard him bitterly.

BARNEY (sarcastic):
Oh! Good morning! You're early!

BRAD:
Hello. Say, I'm sorry I kept you all waiting—

BARNEY (grimly):
Yeah?

BRAD (with enthusiasm):
I got an idea for a new number and lost track of time . . . Got a piano? I'll play it for you.

TRIXIE (rising angrily):
Say, listen kid—*I'm* the comedienne around here. We've had enough of your gags. *They ain't funny!*

Brad notices their coldness, turns to Polly.

POLLY (sharply):
Please stop it, Brad. There's a limit to everything.

Brad is amazed. Barney rises, unsmiling.

BARNEY (gruffly):
I'm locking this office. Get out, everybody—will you?

All rise and start for door, cold-shouldering Brad.

BRAD (to Barney, puzzled):
Don't you want your money?

BARNEY (wheels savagely on Brad):
Say, listen—

Brad takes out bundle of crisp bills. Barney's eyes pop out. Everybody stares, as Brad counts the money.

BRAD (holding money out to Barney):
There you are. Fifteen thousand cash!

Barney, in a trance, unbelieving, takes money and stares at it.

TRIXIE (overjoyed):
Brad, you darling! I always knew you were on the level!

POLLY (hugging Brad):
Brad!

Suddenly Barney slumps over in a dead faint from the shock, the bills fluttering all over the room. Gigolo Eddie looks at Barney with concern, opens a bottle, but instead of applying it to Barney's lips, is about to take a drink himself. Trixie gives him a look, snatches the bottle away from him, looks at Barney, and takes a quick gulp. Polly, Carol, and Brad start picking up the bills. Barney sits up slowly in a daze and looks around him.

FADE OUT

FADE IN

53.   FULL SHOT   BARE STAGE   FROM AUDITORIUM
Pianist pounds out music of "Pettin' in the Park," ensemble number led by Polly and Don, the juvenile. Dance director at footlights is rehearsing them and chorus, all in practice clothes. Barney stands by proscenium watching. Brad watches from side of stage.

DANCE DIRECTOR:
Okay—right into the routine, now, kids—lemme see something!

As Polly and Don finish their duet and exit, chorus goes energetically into intricate dance routine.

54.   BACK STAGE   SIDE ANGLE
Polly and Don enter from stage, breathless. In background, dance director and chorus on stage rehearsing hard.

DANCE DIRECTOR OFF (shouting):
  Hold it! (Piano stops; chorus pauses in dance.) Y'ain't
  got that yet . . . watch me . . . I'll show you the
  steps—slow.

On stage, chorus watches intently as director walks
through routine. Brad walks up to Don and Polly in foreground.

BRAD (to Don, earnestly):
  Listen—Gordon—you've got to get some life into
  it—some punch—some feeling—here's what I
  mean—look—

Brad sings couple of lines of "Pettin' in the Park."

DON (haughtily):
  And what do I do that's so terrible?

BRAD:
  You do this—

Brad sings same lines, imitating Don's manner. Offended, Don stiffens angrily. Barney approaches and
watches Brad appreciatively.

BRAD:
  You don't give!

DON (indignantly):
  Indeed. I know my business. I've been a juvenile for
  eighteen years.

Don turns and stalks away in a huff.

BARNEY (to Brad):
  Yeah, he's been a juvenile for eighteen years—and
  you can't teach him anything.

Barney slips his arm companionably through Brad's and
walks him away. Polly sits on bench adjusting her dancing shoes.

DANCE DIRECTOR OFF:
>Come on—let's try that!

Piano resumes as chorus starts routine again in background.

55.   MED SHOT   BARNEY AND BRAD
Chorus rehearsing in background.

BARNEY (coaxing):
>*You* ought to play the juvenile part. You've got it over Gordon like a tent. Why don't you reconsider, kid? Give your numbers a break.

BRAD:
>No. I've told you, Barney—I *can't*.

BARNEY:
>But why? You never give a reason. You've got a voice, you've got personality, you can do it, and you won't. Why not?

Brad starts to speak, then hesitates and shakes his head stubbornly.

BRAD:
>Let it go at that, Barney. Once and for all, no public appearance.

56.   MED SHOT   POLLY
sitting on bench watching Brad and Barney in background. Beyond them chorus is still rehearsing. Trixie enters unnoticed by Polly and regards latter's intent gaze on Brad.

TRIXIE:
>Listen, honey. You have a big yen for that boy, haven't you?

Polly starts, then smiles, a bit fussed.

POLLY:
>I—like him—of course.

The way she says it means "I love him." Trixie shakes her head somberly. In background Barney shrugs helplessly as Brad walks out of scene.

TRIXIE:
> There's something very funny about him—something *very* mysterious. Look—

Trixie shows Polly newspaper clipping.[7] Polly reads it, frowning.

TRIXIE (as Polly reads):
> Did he ever tell you where he got fifteen thousand dollars? And why he has to live on twenty-five dollars a week, when he can go out and come back with that much money? Now look—Toronto bank clerk took twenty thousand from bank and disappeared—

POLLY:
> I can read.

TRIXIE:
> That's quite a coincidence, I should say.

POLLY:
> What's a coincidence?

TRIXIE (indicating words of clipping with finger):
> New York police asked to check up on Broadway night spots. And here is the description of him—five foot nine—light curly hair—

POLLY (rises angrily):
> That could describe anybody.

TRIXIE:
> Couldn't describe me. Couldn't describe you. And it does describe him. He *is* about five foot nine. And he *has* light hair. And where *did* he get that money?

Polly starts to walk toward dressing rooms, clipping clutched in her hand, worried but trying to dismiss her doubts. Trixie walks beside her, CAMERA TRUCKING with them.

POLLY:
> Don't be ridiculous, Trixie. You're letting your imagination run away with you.

TRIXIE (sincerely):
> Honey, listen, I don't want to see you fall in love with a guy who'll get you into a mess of trouble . . . It's just that I like you—and I'm worried about you and about what may happen.

POLLY (thoughtfully):
> I know—but I'm sure—

TRIXIE (interrupting):
> What are you sure? What do you actually know about him? Where'd he come from? Does he ever talk about himself? Remember he wouldn't sign a check for Barney. Had to be cash. And he won't get out and sing Gordon's part. Why? Afraid that newspaper-men—

Trixie suddenly breaks off as they reach door into corridor leading to dressing room stairs and stage door. She clutches Polly's arm, pointing off. Polly looks, perturbed.

57.   FULL SHOT   STAGE DOOR   FROM POLLY'S ANGLE
Brad is arguing with a young man, who might be a reporter. Man shakes head stubbornly. Brad furtively reaches into his pocket, offers man some bills. Man hesitates, then nods, takes money.

58.   CLOSE SHOT   BRAD AND MAN

BRAD:
> Don't talk. And don't come back here! You promise?

MAN (pocketing money):
> I said I wouldn't, didn't I?

Man exits to street. Brad looks worried.

59.   CLOSE SHOT   POLLY AND TRIXIE

Polly is greatly troubled, Trixie convinced. Polly nervously glances at clipping again.

POLLY (nervously tense):
> Don't say anything to anyone. I'll talk to him, Trixie—
> at lunch. I'll find out—

                                        DISSOLVE TO:

60.   INT. LINDY'S RESTAURANT   DAY
        BRAD AND POLLY AT TABLE
near end of their lunch. Brad is engrossed in discussion of the show. Polly is visibly worried.

BRAD:
> No. Gordon will turn out all right, I'm sure of it.
> Polly, listen, do you think that duet should have
> something where—

Brad starts to hum a few bars. Polly listens abstractedly, her mind on other things.

POLLY (suddenly):
> Were you ever in Toronto, dear?

Brad is surprised and puzzled.

BRAD:
> What? Toronto? (Polly nods.) Yes. I've been there.
> Long time ago.

Polly watches him searchingly. His casual manner might be assumed.

POLLY:
> Trixie thinks she saw you in Toronto.

BRAD:

> That's possible. I was there two years ago. (He looks at watch, starts.) Gosh, my date with the publishers! (He rises, hands her bill.) Here, pay the check, honey—I'm late.

Brad kisses her and hurries out. Ruefully, suspicions unallayed, Polly stares after him. She takes clipping from her purse, looks at it, then after Brad. Slowly she tears the clipping to bits.

FADE OUT

FADE IN

61.   EXT. BILLBOARD   FULL SHOT

Twenty-four sheet announces Barney Hopkins's new all-star revue, "coming soon." Musical background of number from show. FADE IN superimposed multitude of dancing feet and legs. Feet and legs FADE OUT, but music continues, as bill poster slaps up sheet announcing "opens next week."

WIPE OFF TO:

62.   CLOSE-UP   CHATTER COLUMN OF "VARIETY"

> "Barney Hopkins promises some real novelties in his new show due to open Wednesday night."

Music continues. FADE IN superimposed dancing feet and legs.

WIPE OFF TO:

63.   CLOSE-UP   NEWSPAPER ADVERTISEMENT

On theatrical page, proclaiming big opening at certain theater of Barney's show "tomorrow night." FADE IN superimposed dancing feet and legs as music continues.

DISSOLVE TO:

64.   MULTIPLE TRICK SHOT   FEET AND LEGS

filling screen, dancing wildly as background music increases in tempo.

WIPE OFF TO:

65.   EXT. FULL SHOT   THEATER MARQUEE SIGN   NIGHT
blinking on and off: Tonight   World Premiere   Tonight.[8]

PAN DOWN TO:

66.   FULL SHOT—THEATER ENTRANCE
People in full dress flocking into theater.

WIPE OFF TO:

67.   INT. STAGE   FULL SHOT   FROM ABOVE
set for opening number. All bustle, confusion, and nervous tension of opening night. Subdued babble of voices; from beyond curtain come sounds of orchestra tuning instruments. Property men dressing stage. Stagehands gesturing to flyman to raise drop. Members of company in various stages of dress and undress scurry about. Voice of callboy, off, shouts: "Five minutes! "

68.   FLASH   ELECTRICIAN AT SWITCHBOARD
testing dimmers and switches, busy stage in background.

QUICK CUT TO:

69.   FLASH   DANCE DIRECTOR
correcting some steps of Carol and several chorus girls in costume. Carol is ready to lead number.

QUICK CUT TO:

70.   FLASH   LOW ANGLE SHOT   STAGEHAND
on knees amidst confusion, calmly tacking down loose ground cloth, as legs hurry back and forth past him.

QUICK CUT TO:

71.   FLASH   THREE SHOW GIRLS
Excitedly taking turns staring through peephole in curtain to spot spenders in audience.

QUICK CUT TO:

72.   FLASH   FULL SHOT   CHORUS DRESSING ROOM
All excitement, helter-skelter. Dressers helping girls into costumes. Wail of girl who has lost something. Girl helping another make up. Two girls quarreling over ownership of pair of stockings. One girl quietly knitting as she

waits. Callboy's voice, off: "Overture!" Girls redouble
frantic efforts to hurry.

QUICK CUT TO:

73.   FLASH   ORCHESTRA PIT
Musicians in full dress. Orchestra leader takes place, raps
on stand, raises baton. Musicians immediately quiet,
watching him. Leader with sweep of arm starts overture.

QUICK CUT TO:

74.   FLASH   STAGE
Overture playing, off. Stage growing orderly and quiet.
Barney hustles across, last quick glance about to see all is
ready. Worried stage manager rushes up to Barney from
dressing room corridor and whispers in his ear, with excited gestures. With a frown and gasp of dismay, Barney
dashes off toward dressing rooms, stage manager trailing
after him.

QUICK CUT TO:

75.   INT. DRESSING ROOM
Overture music distantly in background. Trixie, Polly,
and Brad with long faces are assembled about rubbing
table, watching Gigolo Eddie, with sleeves rolled up,
pound at Don Gordon, juvenile, lying on the table. He is
rubbing him with liquid from an open bottle of gin.

DON (in agony):
Ooooooooh!

GIGOLO EDDIE:
This stuff is just as good to rub with as it is to drink.
It penetrates. Show me the spot.

DON (groans):
Been rubbing me for an hour—and now he says
show me the spot!

Barney enters greatly worried.

BARNEY:
What is this?

All shake heads lugubriously.

GIGOLO EDDIE:
His lumbago![9]

Barney shoves Eddie aside.

BARNEY (to Don):
Stand up!

DON (writhing):
I can't stand up. Oooooh!

BARNEY:
Oh, you can't stand up, can't you?

Barney grabs Don by shoulder, pulls him off table, and stands him up. Don at once groans and bends over double.

DON (wailing):
I can't—I can't!

BARNEY:
Straighten up, you little weasel!

DON:
Ouch! I can't, I tell you!

Barney pounds and shakes Don, raving at him.

BARNEY:
You don't think you're going out to sing a love song with your back doubled up, do you? What kind of a love song do you think this is? You got to straighten up. You got to stop being a baby. Mind over matter. Mind over matter.

Don tries to straighten up, then doubles over again with a groan, sitting down weakly. Barney stands over Don, berating him.

BARNEY (fiercely):
I got a show. I spent weeks—months—getting a show

together. I worked—I slaved! Opening night! We open tonight—and you've got lumbago!

Barney yanks Don to his feet again. With a terrific groan the juvenile collapses in Barney's hands and slides to the floor. Barney regards him with disgust, then gives up hope with shrug of despair and turns away, to stage manager, sarcastically.

BARNEY:
Go announce the show won't open. Give back their money! Tell 'em our juvenile is dying of old age! (Sees Brad, comes to life.) Say, listen to me, kid. It's up to you. *Now* you've *got* to do it!

Stage manager turns back to door. Brad regards him frowning. Barney catches his arm.

BARNEY (forcefully):
You've got to go on in his place!

BRAD (positively):
I can't do that, Barney.

All cluster round Brad.

BARNEY:
What do you mean you can't? The curtain is ready to go up. There's a show going on. Your money is in it—you've got to go out and do it.

BRAD (shaking his head):
There's a reason why—

BARNEY:
There is *no* reason— (Brad shrugs.) All right—what's your reason?

Brad closes his lips firmly and turns away without reply. Trixie steps up to Brad and faces him as the others draw away hopelessly.

TRIXIE:

>Listen. I don't care even if you have to go to jail after this performance. You ought to forget about yourself and do it anyway. Do you know what this means—if the show doesn't go on? It means that all those girls in this show—all those poor kids who threw up jobs—and who'll never get other jobs in these times— all those kids been living on nothing—starving themselves these five weeks we've been rehearsing— hoping for this show to go on—and be a success— They're depending on you! You can't let them down—you can't—if you do—God knows what will happen to those girls— They'll have to do things I wouldn't want on *my* conscience. And it'll be on *yours*— You can go out and sing Gordon's part and put this show over—and if you don't—I don't care what the reason is—

Brad looks at Trixie, then at Polly, wavering in his decision.

POLLY (catching his arm):

>She's right, Brad, *I* don't care what the reason is.

BRAD (thoughtfully):

>I hadn't thought about it that way. (He pauses. All look at him hopefully. With sudden decision.) Yes, of course, I'll do it!

There is a general gasp of delight.

BARNEY (greatly excited):

>Come on! (To stage manager.) Help the kid with his make-up. He doesn't go on for the first seven minutes. We don't have to hold the curtain. Come on.

Barney hustles Brad out with stage manager, who picks up costume on way.

76.   FULL SHOT   DRESSING ROOM CORRIDOR

as Barney shoves stage manager and Brad into dressing

room down hall, then dashes off toward stage. Polly and Trixie in doorway look after Brad.

POLLY (worried):
> Gee! If anything happens to him now, we're responsible. We are.

TRIXIE (with enthusiasm):
> Say, there's more to that kid than I thought there was. He has nerve. He's regular. He *belongs* in the show business—

POLLY:
> He's risking going to prison—for us.

TRIXIE:
> I like that kid. If he goes to prison for this, I'll visit him there . . . (Pause.) Well, at least I'll write to him once in a while.

Stage manager comes out and hurries toward stage.

POLLY (with sudden decision):
> I want to see him—and let him know *I know* what it means.

Polly goes rapidly to door of room where Brad entered, knocks and enters.

77. INT. BRAD'S DRESSING ROOM
Polly enters, looks admiringly at Brad who is finishing dressing. He looks at her, shrugs, and grins ruefully.

POLLY:
> Brad, it's wonderful of you to take this chance. It's— it's courageous.

BRAD:
> It's not courageous exactly. Say, but how do you know? *Do* you know?

POLLY (nods):
> Oh, but don't think about it, Brad. Just think about—

I love you and always will . . . No matter what happens—

BRAD (taking her in his arms):
Polly—honey—

POLLY (snuggles in his arms):
After tonight—you can tell me all about it—I'll understand and maybe I can help—

BRAD (draws back, puzzled):
After tonight—?

A knock comes at door.

CALLBOY OFF:
Brad Roberts on stage—Polly Parker on stage!

Brad and Polly come down to earth with a thud and start
breathlessly for door.

BRAD:
Wish us luck, sweetheart.

POLLY:
I do. I do. I wish us luck!

They pause for a kiss, then run out.

DISSOLVE TO:

78. FULL SHOT   STAGE
as curtain rises on production number, "Pettin' in the
Park," led by Brad and Polly, with full chorus backing
them up.[10]

"Pettin' in the Park"
(Chorus)
Pettin' in the park—(bad boy)
Pettin' in the dark—(bad girl)
First you pet a little, let up a little
And then you get a little kiss.
Pettin' on the sly—(oh my)
Act a little shy—(aw why)
Struggle just a little then hug a little

And cuddle up and whisper this—
Come on, I've been waiting long—
Why don't we get started—
Come on, maybe this is wrong,
But gee, what of it—We just love it.
Pettin' in the park—(bad boy)
Pettin' in the dark—(bad girl)
What you doin' honey, I feel so funny,
I'm pettin' in the park with you.

Curtain falls at end of number to great burst of enthusiastic applause.

QUICK CUT TO:

79. FLASH   AUDIENCE AND STAGE
Audience applauding as Brad and Polly take curtain call.

DISSOLVE TO:

80. CLOSE-UP   PROGRAM
as hands turn page and finger indicates "Intermission."

DISSOLVE TO:

81. INT. THEATER LOBBY
as ushers open doors and men and women flock out for smokes, chattering enthusiastically about show. Two critics meet, light cigarettes, third joins them, is introduced, and borrows cigarette.

FIRST CRITIC:
Who is the boy?

SECOND CRITIC:
Brad Roberts according to the announcement—and the program says he's done most of the music. Smart kid!

THIRD CRITIC:
Something very familiar about him. I've seen him—

not in the theater either. Wait a minute. Let me have a nickel.

With sour look first critic hands third critic a coin.

THIRD CRITIC (hurrying off):
I'm going to find out if—

DISSOLVE TO:

82. FLASH   CLOSE SHOT   CRITIC (THIRD) IN PHONE BOOTH nodding and asking questions in growing excitement. We cannot hear him through closed door of booth, but can see his suspicions are being confirmed.

DISSOLVE TO:

83. THEATER LOBBY   TWO CRITICS
First critic jotting notes on back of envelope, as third critic rushes up to them, whispers triumphantly in ear of second critic.

SECOND CRITIC (incredulous):
I can't believe it.

THIRD CRITIC (confidentially):
The description! And I knew I'd seen him before . . . We'll go back and get Barney to tell us the truth. What a front page story that will make.[11]

Doorman in background announces "Second Act," people in lobby drifting into theater as critics turn away.

DISSOLVE TO:

84. FULL SHOT   STAGE
as auditorium lights dim and curtain rises on Carol's "Remember My Forgotten Man" number.[12] She stands by lamppost in rain. As she sings, we see panorama in background of Bonus Army marching. Tramp of marching feet comes through music. Men's voices join Carol's in last chorus.

"Remember My Forgotten Man"
(Chorus)
Remember my forgotten man
You put a rifle in his hand
You sent him far away
You shouted "Hip Hooray"
But look at him today—
Remember my forgotten man
You had him cultivate the land
He walked behind a plow
The sweat fell from his brow
But look at him right now—
And once he used to love me
I was happy then—
He used to take care of me
Won't you bring him back again—
Cause ever since the world began—
A woman's got to have a man
Forgetting him, you see, means
You're forgetting me
Like my forgotten man.

As number ends,

FADE OUT

FADE IN
85.   CLOSE-UP   NEWSPAPER PICTURE
Brad's head and shoulders, no caption visible.

CAROL'S VOICE OFF (excited):
    Polly—look at this! *Look at this!*

POLLY'S VOICE OFF (breathless):
    Gosh. Oh, I can't believe it!

TRUCK BACK TO:

86.   CLOSE-UP   FRONT PAGE OF NEWSPAPER
held in Carol's hands.

POLLY'S VOICE OFF (continues in amazement):
Oh, I never *dreamed* of such a thing!

Picture, caption, headlines, and part of sensational news story are visible.

"BRAD ROBERTS" REALLY ROBERT TREAT BRADFORD!

Blue Blood Millions Helped Finance Musical Comedy Hit

Believed to be following technical studies at Stevens Institute, Robert Treat Bradford, son of one of Boston's oldest and wealthiest families, has for some time been living close to Broadway under an assumed name as a struggling songwriter, etc., etc.

87. FULL SHOT GIRLS' LIVING ROOM
Polly and Carol devouring story in newspaper. Trixie crowds in and looks over their shoulders.

TRIXIE (vehemently):
I always knew that kid was somebody. You can't fool me much.

POLLY:
Why, Trixie Lorraine, you thought I was a fool to have anything to do with him!

TRIXIE:
Say, you don't know when I'm kidding, do you?

Brad bursts into the room. Polly runs to him.

TRIXIE (greeting him):
Here's the social lion, himself.

POLLY:
Oh, Brad—why didn't you tell me? Why did you let me think—

She breaks off.

BRAD:
>Think what?

TRIXIE (covering up):
>We thought you'd murdered a man!

BRAD:
>Well, you see, my family—my brother particularly—is one of those Back Bay Boston Blue Bloods—

TRIXIE:
>Back Bay Boston Blue Bloods— Say that quickly. *Try* to say it quickly. Back-Bay-Boston-Blue-Bloods.

CAROL:
>Trixie, just try to relax a minute. So what, Brad?

BRAD:
>Well, he didn't want me to go on with my music— He has no use for the theater—or anybody connected with it. It's the old plot— He must have read it in a book. *My* family, *my* social background, *I* mustn't breathe the same air with show girls.

TRIXIE (belligerently):
>What do you mean—show girls? Get down to cases!

BRAD:
>That's what my Big Blue-Blooded Back Bay Brother calls anyone in the theater. Show girls.

CAROL:
>Nice fellow—your brother! Tolerant!

BRAD (worried):
>Oh, he's all right in his way, but I know there's going to be a battle. If I hadn't sung in the show, no one would have known Brad Roberts.

POLLY:
>He'll be proud of you now. Anyone would.

BRAD (ruefully):
   I'll soon know about *that*. He's waiting for me now.

With a glance at his watch, Brad crosses to door. Polly accompanies him.

BRAD (to Polly):
   Where'll you be in the afternoon?

POLLY:
   Right here until show time.

BRAD (to Polly):
   I'll call you.

He snatches a quick kiss and turns to go.

CAROL (to Brad):
   Don't let him bluff you about show girls. Tell him he doesn't even know what a show girl is.

Brad goes out. Trixie calls after him from door.

TRIXIE:
   Tell him there are good people in the theater—just as good as any Back Bay Boston Blue-Blooded Block-heads.

She smacks the *B*'s, closes the door.[13]

> DISSOLVE TO:

88.   FLASH   EXT. IMPOSING CLUB ENTRANCE   DAY
Dignified carving above door, University Club. Stiff, uniformed doorman on steps.

> DISSOLVE TO:

89.   INT. CLUB LOUNGE   FULL SHOT
sedately silent. Elderly men sit about reading high-brow magazines and papers—*North American Review, Manchester Guardian, Town and Country, London Times*, etc. Others sit doing nothing, but clear their throats politely at intervals. Noiseless servants glide about in respectful attendance. A man laughs. All turn, regarding him with indignant disapproval.

90.   CLOSE SHOT   MAN WHO LAUGHED
Other men in background regarding him indignantly.
Man shrivels, looks around apologetically, then at maga-
zine in hands.

INSERT   CLOSE-UP   MAGAZINE
Foreign Affairs
with copy of *Ballyhoo* tucked in it.

BACK TO SCENE:
Embarrassed man tries to hide *Ballyhoo* by turning other
magazine pages hastily, without others seeing him do it,
his discomfort obvious.

91.   FULL SHOT   CORNER OF LOUNGE
J. Lawrence Bradford, Brad's older brother, and Faneuil
Hall Peabody,[14] the Bradford family lawyer, sit side by side
on huge leather davenport, frowning as they reread
newspaper articles.

INSERT   CLOSE-UP   CHATTER COLUMN
"Bobby Bradford, of the Boston social
register Bradfords, backs Hopkins's new
show to put over pretty Polly Parker—
late of the chorus. A break for little Polly
. . . Who said depression?"

BACK TO SCENE:
With angry snort of disgust, J. Lawrence throws down
paper. Peabody follows suit, throws down his paper,
echoing J. Lawrence's snort. Both sit, waiting impatiently.
They talk in properly subdued tones.

J. LAWRENCE (severely):
He's late.

PEABODY (nods weightily):
Fifteen minutes. (As if it were fifteen hours.)

J. LAWRENCE:
We should dispose of this in time to get the noon
train back.

PEABODY (regarding his watch gravely):
 If not, there is the merchants' train at one.

J. LAWRENCE (seriously regarding his own watch):
 New York time?

PEABODY:
 No, Boston time.

J. Lawrence nods gravely, snaps watch shut, and returns heirloom to his pocket. Peabody likewise stows his watch away. J. Lawrence taps arm of davenport with impatient fingers. As Brad enters, J. Lawrence and Peabody rise punctiliously.

J. LAWRENCE (stiffly):
 Good morning, Robert. You are late.

BRAD:
 Not much, am I?

PEABODY (consulting watch):
 Seventeen minutes.

BRAD (with a grin):
 Hello, Peabody.

PEABODY:
 Good morning, young man.

J. LAWRENCE:
 I'll come directly to the point, Robert. (Brad nods and sits.) Your family is greatly disturbed over what has occurred. I hope you appreciate the fact I flew here this morning in bad weather.

Brad starts to say something. J. Lawrence silences him with a gesture and sits opposite him.

J. LAWRENCE (continues earnestly):
 As trustee of your estate and your elder brother, I represent the family in saying that we cannot have you mixed up in this theater business. You know how we feel.

PEABODY (before Brad can speak):
Your mother is greatly concerned and all the members of the family. (He sits, also facing Brad.) I cannot begin to describe to you, my dear boy, the extent of the shock—

BRAD (sincerely):
I'm sorry everybody in the family is shocked, but I'd better come directly to the point, too. Music is my career—you know that!

J. LAWRENCE (interrupting):
Music, yes, but—

BRAD (earnestly):
I mean the kind of music that's sung in shows and over the radio and on records. I don't mean the kind of music played by the Boston Symphony Orchestra. You have to be dead to compose that. I want to write this other kind of music; this show was my big opportunity, the show has clicked, I've got my start, and I'm going on with it. As to my appearing in the show, I know how you feel about that, and I did the best I could to stay out of it. But an emergency came up, I had to do it, and now I can't let them down. Besides, I like it.

J. LAWRENCE (with condescension):
I—uh—I cannot sympathize with your point of view, but I can understand it. Much as the family regrets that one who bears the family name should go in for this sort of sensational career in preference to banking, nevertheless, we have agreed not to oppose you. One thing though we must and will insist upon.

BRAD (getting his back up):
And what's that?

J. LAWRENCE:
This girl—this show girl—whose name is linked with yours—

PEABODY:
Polly Parker.

BRAD (scowling dangerously):
What of it?

J. LAWRENCE (astonished):
What of it? Simply this—

BRAD (interrupting, heatedly):
Listen, before you say anything about her, you better know this—I'm in love with Polly Parker—and I'm going to marry her—if she'll have me!

J. LAWRENCE (explosively):
What!?

His loud exclamation causes all heads to turn. He is the target for a broadside of disapproving looks. The elderly gentleman straightens up in his chair and shakes his head reprovingly.

ELDERLY GENTLEMAN (to the world in general):
I'm going to complain to the house committee.

He subsides again in his chair. J. Lawrence and Peabody stare incredulously at Brad, who nods stubbornly.

BRAD:
Just what I said—

J. LAWRENCE (outraged):
You, marry this cheap little show girl—

BRAD:
Listen, that's pretty much of an old-fashioned idea. Families don't interfere with love affairs nowadays . . . (pause) and if they do, it doesn't mean anything.

J. Lawrence rises with dignity.

J. LAWRENCE:
If you marry that girl, you will not get one cent of income. I don't have to remind you that until you're

thirty, I have the absolute legal right to cut off your income.

BRAD (bluntly):
I understand. And if that's what you wanted to see me about, you're wasting your time. (Abruptly.) I've got more important things to do.

He says this loudly, turns on his heel, and stamps out. Elderly gentleman stiffens up.

ELDERLY GENTLEMAN (plaintively):
I shall certainly complain to the house committee.

J. Lawrence looks after Brad in shocked surprise, sits down shaking his head.

J. LAWRENCE (seething):
I can't believe it. He never talked to me like that before. That's from associating with these cheap people.

PEABODY (leans close, confidentially):
It's the girl. I know these show girls. They're just little parasites, little gold diggers. This girl is behind everything he says. She wants—I know exactly what she wants—she wants to get her hands into the Bradford millions . . . Mark my word.

J. LAWRENCE:
I don't doubt it. The thing to do is—let's figure on the four o'clock train—(he rises, purposefully) and let's now—

PEABODY (rising):
Let us now what?

J. LAWRENCE:
See this Parker girl.

PEABODY (dubious at once):
I advise against it.

J. LAWRENCE (disregarding Peabody's remark):
If necessary, buy her off.

PEABODY (shakes head apprehensively):
  I suggest we exercise caution—conduct negotiations
  from afar.

J. Lawrence pays no attention, concentrating on his problem. Peabody continues reminiscently, growing almost
wistful as he remembers.

PEABODY (continuing):
  I remember, in my early youth, I trod the primrose
  path on the Great White Way. There I learned the bitter truth that all women of the theater are chiselers,
  parasites, or—as we called them then—gold diggers.
  I remember well one experience I had with a woman
  of the theater. (He sits, with smile of recollection.) It
  was after the big Harvard game, we came down, a
  stout company of young blades, out to learn about
  life. I met this girl at the stage door of the Old Ca-
  sino. We went to Rector's for a bite. I had a cold bird
  and bottle. She nibbled at a steak. Her name was
  Eunice. She called me Fuffy. I don't remember why
  she did, but she called me Fuffy.

J. LAWRENCE (interrupting decisively):
  I'm going to see her.

PEABODY (startled):
  I don't know where she is now. That was thirty years
  ago.

J. LAWRENCE:
  No, no, I mean this Polly Parker woman!

PEABODY (rises):
  Oh . . . ! I wouldn't. I wouldn't go to see her.

J. Lawrence turns, starts away. Peabody lumbers after
him, three steps behind him, his protests growing louder
as they cross the room, to the great indignation of all the
gentlemen present.

PEABODY (continuing with increasing vigor):
> I wouldn't go to see her. You put yourself in her hands. They're parasites, they're blackmailers, they're gold diggers—

As J. Lawrence and Peabody depart, the elderly gentleman stands up outraged.

ELDERLY GENTLEMAN:
> *I resign!*

All the other gentlemen stare at him aghast.

FADE OUT

FADE IN

92. INT. BEDROOM   NEW APARTMENT[15]   FULL SHOT
Carol in teddies, pulling on stockings as she dresses. Through open bathroom door Trixie's head and naked shoulders are visible as she sits in bathtub, humming cheerfully to herself as she scrubs. Both look up at sound of knock at door of living room off.

CAROL (calls, off):
> Come in.

She rises, slipping into negligee.

93. FULL SHOT   LIVING ROOM   NEW APARTMENT
J. Lawrence and Peabody enter empty room, exchange disapproving looks at such unconventionality. They stand looking about uneasily.

94. BATHROOM   NEW APARTMENT
Trixie cranes head curiously from tub.

TRIXIE (calling, off):
> Well, who is it?

J. LAWRENCE'S VOICE OFF (dignified):
> I am J. Lawrence Bradford.

Trixie reacts in surprise.

95.   LIVING ROOM   NEW APARTMENT
Carol enters from bedroom, leaving door ajar. She is in revealing negligee over her underthings, which is not missed by Peabody and J. Lawrence.

J. LAWRENCE (bowing stiffly):
I've come to see Miss Polly Parker.

CAROL (puzzled):
Yes?

J. LAWRENCE:
I am the brother of Robert Treat Bradford, whom you probably know as Brad Roberts.

CAROL (a bit fussed):
Oh, Brad's brother. Sit down. I'll be dressed in just a minute. (She starts out.)

J. LAWRENCE (formally):
Don't bother, Miss Parker. (Carol stares.) I can say what I have to say—

CAROL (interrupting):
But I'm not—

J. LAWRENCE (interrupting):
Please, Miss Parker—

96.   CLOSE SHOT   TRIXIE   IN BATHTUB   NEW APARTMENT
listening with great interest, nodding to herself wisely.

J. LAWRENCE'S VOICE OFF (continuing):
. . . I have just spoken to my brother. He tells me he wants to marry you.

Trixie gulps in surprise.

CAROL'S VOICE OFF:
But you're making a mistake—please let me explain.

97.   LIVING ROOM   NEW APARTMENT

J. LAWRENCE (waving away her protest):
> Don't bother to explain. I've told him that if he dis-
> graces the family by marrying a show girl the family
> is through with him—

CAROL (resenting his manner):
> Did you say *disgrace* the family by marrying a *show
> girl?*

J. LAWRENCE (nods):
> I said exactly that. Show girls are—are—reputed to
> be—parasites, chiselers, gold diggers!

J. Lawrence pauses at a loss for words. Carol burns, starts
to speak angrily. Peabody interrupts.

PEABODY (attempting to conciliate her):
> Show girls are excellent in their way—attractive crea-
> tures—even fascinating—but hardly fitted to shine
> in the upper social circles.

98.   BATHROOM   TRIXIE   IN TUB   NEW APARTMENT
listening but a bit bored. She starts to scrub again. Soap
spurts out of her hands onto floor. She reaches for it. J.
Lawrence's voice comes over this scene.

J. LAWRENCE'S VOICE OFF:
> This is not directed against you personally, Miss Par-
> ker—

99.   MED. CLOSE SHOT   J. LAWRENCE, CAROL, AND PEABODY
LIVING ROOM   NEW APARTMENT

CAROL (sarcastic):
> Oh, no, I understand, not personally. *All* show girls
> are chiselers, and parasites and gold diggers—

J. LAWRENCE (without humor):
> Exactly. And now, Miss Parker—

CAROL (interrupting):
   You'd better let me tell you—

J. LAWRENCE (interrupting in his turn):
   Just tell me—*how much?*

CAROL:
   How much what?

J. LAWRENCE:
   What is your price?

Carol looks at him surprised and angry, speechless.

PEABODY (explicitly):
   How much do you want for releasing his brother
   from his promise to marry you?

CAROL (a harsh little laugh):
   This is very funny.

J. LAWRENCE (earnestly):
   I see nothing amusing in it, Miss Parker. Please—
   don't let's waste time. How much?

CAROL (with admirable restraint):
   I'm sorry.

J. LAWRENCE:
   Sorry?

CAROL (sharply):
   No price on me.

J. LAWRENCE (with grim impatience):
   I insist, Miss Parker, you must have a price. I am in-
   clined to be generous in the matter. (Not a word
   from Carol.) After all, I realize that Bob is a head-
   strong boy, but I'm in charge of him, and I feel I
   know what is best for him.

Carol, burning up, stares at J. Lawrence, wanting to slap
his face. Then holding herself in check turns away sharply.

100.   INT. BEDROOM   NEW APARTMENT
Trixie, hurrying into her clothes, is almost dressed. She listens, a firm resolve on her face.

101.   INT. LIVING ROOM   NEW APARTMENT
Carol, her patience at an end, turns on J. Lawrence.

CAROL (fiercely):
Say, I've heard about enough. If you don't mind—

Carol walks toward hall door, with evident intention of opening it and showing them out. At this moment Trixie barges in, pretends coy dismay.

TRIXIE:
Oh, I beg your pardon. Am I interrupting?

CAROL:
No. (Introducing her formally.) This is Mr. Bradford, Brad's brother.

TRIXIE (sweetly):
Charmed.

CAROL (burnt up):
Beware! Trixie is a show girl.

Peabody takes a breathless eyeful. Trixie gushes as she eyes him.

TRIXIE:
And who is this distinguished looking man?

CAROL:
I don't know.

PEABODY:
My name is Peabody—Faneuil H. Peabody.

TRIXIE:
Faneuil?

PEABODY:
Faneuil.

TRIXIE (patting his arm):
    When I know you better I'll call you Fanny. (She sits,
    beckons Peabody.) Have you a cigarette?

Peabody holds out gold case to her. Trixie takes a cigarette, then holds Peabody's hand while she stares at case.

TRIXIE (in awed tones):
    Gold!

She takes case from Peabody, inspects it admiringly, smiles
at Peabody, then, absentmindedly, hands him back cigarette, keeping case. Peabody looks disturbed. Trixie
catches his look, laughs.

TRIXIE:
    Oh, my error. (Returns case, takes cigarette again.)
    Light, please.

Peabody awkwardly stows case away in pocket and prof-
fers Trixie platinum and gold lighter. She holds his hand
as she gets light, eyeing lighter.

TRIXIE (giving him the works):
    Your hand is shaking.

Peabody gulps; she manages to let her knee touch his.
Trixie leans back smiling coquettishly up at Peabody.

TRIXIE (sighing comfortably):
    Well! What an unexpected pleasure. Sit down, won't
    you?

She reaches up, pulls his hand. With a helpless look at J.
Lawrence, Peabody sinks down on couch beside Trixie.

CAROL (an edge on her voice):
    They—that is Mr. Bradford—wants me to give up
    Brad. (She winks quickly at Trixie.) Says we're all
    chiselers and gold diggers—and he wants to know
    my price.

TRIXIE:
    Have you told him—*Polly?*

CAROL:
I was about to tell him where to head in.

TRIXIE (quickly):
Oh, I wouldn't be hasty.

J. LAWRENCE (worried):
I'd at least discuss it further. After all, we are grown up—sensible. You're a woman of the world—I'm a man of the world.

TRIXIE (eagerly):
We should have a conference. (Affectionately, leaning close to Peabody, taking his hand.) Isn't that what businessmen have—when they're away from home—conferences?

She flickers her eyelids at Peabody who stares fascinated.

TRIXIE (with growing enthusiasm):
Listen. I know a new speakie—just opened—their liquor is good—and I know good liquor. (Jumps to her feet.) It's right around the corner and we'll be with you in just two minutes. I'll just slip into something—pardon me.

Trixie reaches behind Peabody for something he's sitting on. He rises, picks it up, hands it to her.

PEABODY:
What's this?

TRIXIE (holds it up; Peabody gapes):
Slip. (To Carol.) Come on, honey. Let's not keep them waiting. (To the men.) Amuse yourselves. We'll just be a minute.

Trixie comes back, picks up magazines, hands one to J. Lawrence.

TRIXIE:
Here's something to read, Mr. Bradford. (Handing

other to Peabody.) And here's some pictures to look at— (hesitates, then smiles sweetly) Fanny.

Trixie turns and hurries out with Carol. Peabody and J. Lawrence, magazines in limp hands, stare after the departed damsels, then turn and exchange worried looks. Peabody shakes his head in pessimistic apprehension. J. Lawrence shrugs angrily, looks at magazine in hand, chucks it irritably down on the table, wipes sweat from forehead, crosses, and opens window for breath of air. He begins to pace up and down. Peabody uncomfortably starts to speak, changes his mind, slumps in chair, and begins to peruse magazine.

102.   INT. BEDROOM   NEW APARTMENT
Trixie is urging Carol to dress. Carol sits stubbornly shaking head, fuming in anger.

CAROL:
    I'm not going.

TRIXIE:
    Don't be dumb! This is the first fun I've had since grandma got her toe caught in the mousetrap.

CAROL (rising):
    I'm going to tell him the truth and throw him out!

TRIXIE:
    After what he called you—a parasite! Say, what is a parasite? You better resent it!

CAROL (mad):
    He *did* get under my skin. The stuck-up snob!

TRIXIE (pleading):
    They've had their turn. Now let's have ours! Let's take them for a ride. Use the bathroom while I use the phone. (To herself as she dials.) Pennsylvania 4–0–62. (To Carol.) We'll let those guys pay for their fun—right through the checkbook.

Carol nods emphatically, says to herself, "It's coming to them," and starts to undress, going into the bathroom. Trixie turns smiling to phone.

TRIXIE (into phone, quickly):
Hello—is this Madame Minnie? This is Miss Trixie Lorraine. That hat you know—with the—yes—no, the expensive one—

Carol continues making her hasty toilette, as Trixie phones.

103.   INT. LIVING ROOM
J. Lawrence is walking up and down, frowning thoughtfully. Peabody sits looking at magazine with great interest. He chuckles in amusement. J. Lawrence notices Peabody's mirth, comes over, and stares down, disapprovingly expecting to see "art" studies. His face registers surprise.

INSERT   CLOSE SHOT   MAGAZINE IN PEABODY'S HANDS
It is a copy of *Town and Country*. Peabody is laughing over a picture of a litter of puppies.

BACK TO SCENE:
J. Lawrence turns away, again paces the room. A knock at the door causes them to look up, uncertain whether or not to answer it. They exchange perplexed looks. A moment later Trixie enters, fastening herself together, not fully dressed, crosses, and opens the door. A messenger boy, hatbox in hand, stands there.

TRIXIE (pretending surprise):
What's this?

MESSENGER (stepping inside):
C.O.D. for Miss Polly Parker—seventy-five bucks.

J. Lawrence and Peabody watch uncomfortably. Trixie shakes her head mournfully as she opens box, takes out hat, and holds it up.

TRIXIE:

Seventy-five! Just for a little hat! Oh, but she will
look so adorable in it, won't she? (J. Lawrence does
not answer.) Yes . . . she will. Let me see now . . .
(To boy, naively.) What does C.O.D. mean?

MESSENGER:

Means you got to pay for it.

TRIXIE:

Oh, how inconvenient. Well, take it back. (Begins to
repack hat, regretfully; sweetly.) Oh, dear, she will
be in such a bad mood!

J. LAWRENCE:

Who will?

TRIXIE:

Polly.

Once again she unwraps hat and holds it up so men cannot help seeing it as she talks on.

TRIXIE (continuing):

She did so want to wear this hat when she went to
lunch with you. And when she doesn't get what she
wants—Oh dear—you don't know Polly—she gets
so disagreeable! Sits—and won't say anything—no
fun at all—won't agree with anything you say. She
probably won't even go out with us . . . We three
will just have to go alone.

She returns hat to box, shrugging sadly.

TRIXIE (to messenger handing back box):

Run along.

Messenger looks puzzled, starts to go. J. Lawrence stops
him quickly.

J. LAWRENCE:

Just a minute. How much is it?

MESSENGER:
> Seventy-five bucks.

J. LAWRENCE:
> Seventy-five—for a hat!

MESSENGER:
> Sure. That's what the ticket calls for.

J. LAWRENCE (with sudden decision):
> Here. Leave the hat.

MESSENGER (wearily):
> Okay.

With relief, the messenger hands box to J. Lawrence and swaggers out. Trixie, eyes glistening, takes box from J. Lawrence.

TRIXIE (gushing):
> Oh, you darling man! Polly will love you for this.

She places box on table, starts to unpack hat again as Carol enters.

TRIXIE:
> Polly, darling, this sweet big brother of Brad's has insisted on paying for your hat.

CAROL:
> Oh, he mustn't do that.

TRIXIE:
> Oh, but he has.

CAROL:
> Oh, but I couldn't.

Trixie tries hat on Carol. Two men watch. J. Lawrence, in spite of himself, is struck by Carol's loveliness, and effectiveness of hat.

TRIXIE:
Oh, but you must. It looks adorable on you. (To
men.) Doesn't it?

They nod vaguely. Trixie steps back, head on side, studying effect.

TRIXIE (to Carol):
All you need now is a corsage. Lilies of the valley
and gardenias. And I shall want orchids. Let's send
for them.

J. LAWRENCE (uncomfortably):
Let's be going. I must get a four o'clock train to Boston.

TRIXIE:
I'm very sorry, Mr. Bradford, but I couldn't leave the
room without a corsage. And I wouldn't let Polly—I
just couldn't let her go out that way.

J. LAWRENCE:
We'll buy you a corsage—on the way. Only let's hurry.

TRIXIE:
Oh, he's a darling. So generous.

There comes another knock at door. Trixie starts for bedroom.

TRIXIE:
Carol, will you answer that. I *must* powder my nose.

Trixie hurries out. Carol opens door. Another messenger
boy stands there carrying hatbox.

CAROL (pretending surprise):
What's this?

J. Lawrence and Peabody, after sight of boy, exchange
worried looks.

BOY (stuttering):
Th—th—the—this—is a—a—

PEABODY:
> Looks like another hat. (To boy, officiously.) We *have* a hat, my lad.

BOY:
> B—b—b—but—

PEABODY:
> You must have the wrong address—

BOY (shakes head, positively):
> N—n—n—no.

CAROL (taking hatbox):
> Who is the hat for?

BOY:
> F—f—f—for M—m—Miss T—T—T Trixie Lorraine.

CAROL (taking box to table):
> Oh, for Trixie.

Peabody looks helplessly at J. Lawrence, who frowns as Carol quickly opens box and takes out hat.

CAROL:
> Oh, let's see it. (Holding it up.) Oh, how ducky.

Peabody questions J. Lawrence with a look. J. Lawrence nods grimly. Peabody sighs, puts hand into his pocket.

PEABODY (to boy):
> How much?

BOY:
> It's ss—s—s—

PEABODY (annoyed):
> Let me see the bill. (Boy hands it to him.) Seventy-five dollars! Do *all* hats cost seventy-five dollars?

J. LAWRENCE:
> Strange, isn't it? A bit of cloth, a strip of ribbon, a feather—

Peabody dejectedly hands boy bills. Boy looks in pockets for change.

CAROL (effusively):
> Oh, you dear sweet man. You're not paying for it. You're *not*. (Calling excitedly.) Trixie! Come in, Trixie!

BOY:
> I d—d—don't know if I can make ch—ch—change.

CAROL:
> How much?

BOY:
> F—f—five dollars.

CAROL (generously, to Peabody):
> Oh, let him keep the change. (To boy, not allowing Peabody to speak.) Buy yourself a yacht.

Boy grins and ducks out. Trixie enters.

CAROL (to Trixie):
> Look at the darling hat. (Indicates Peabody.) *Handsome* bought it for you.

TRIXIE (takes hat, removing one on her head):
> Oh, the sweet man! He shouldn't have paid for it. (But trying it on.) Oh, what a pretty hat! (Smiling archly at Peabody.) You *do* like me in it, don't you? (Peabody nods, speechless.) You *don't* think I'm extravagant, do you?

Peabody continues to nod in stupefied manner. Trixie puts her arm through his, and starts to pilot him toward door.

TRIXIE (with enthusiasm):
> You know, we must take a stroll on Fifth Avenue after lunch and look at the shops. You'd be surprised how reasonable things are these days.

Peabody looks at her in speechless alarm as they go out.

Carol has straightened hat before mirror as J. Lawrence
waits impatiently.

CAROL (turning to J. Lawrence):
　　Trixie says I look adorable. I don't, do I? What do
　　you think?

She slips her arm through his, smiling at him affectionately.

J. LAWRENCE (dignified, as they start out):
　　My mind is on other things, Miss Parker.

CAROL (sweetly):
　　Call me—Polly.

J. Lawrence regards her startled. Carol halts, pouting.

CAROL:
　　Please! (Smiles invitingly.) Say it now—"Polly"—or
　　I won't go another step . . .

J. LAWRENCE (as if taking medicine):
　　Very well—*Polly*.

Happily, Carol snuggles close and they start out. J. Lawrence looks dazed.

　　　　　　　　　　　　　　　　　　　　DISSOLVE TO:

104.　　INT. SPEAKEASY　CLOSE SHOT　TABLE FOR FOUR
Half emptied plate of sandwiches, ashtray full of cigarette
stubs, crumpled napkins, and emptied champagne glasses
show "luncheon" has been in progress for some time.
Couple of boxes containing new perfume bottles by girls'
places. Waiter's hand refills glasses with champagne. Two
girls' hands quickly pick up glasses; two men's hands
take glasses more hesitantly. Background noise of chatter,
laughter, and clink of glasses.

　　　　　　　　　　　　　　　　　　　　TRUCK BACK TO:

105.　　FULL SHOT　GROUP AT TABLE
as they down champagne. Several boxes of stockings,
gloves, etc., obviously just purchased, are by chairs. Carol

and Trixie enjoying situation, Peabody nervous, J. Lawrence still urging a settlement.

J. LAWRENCE (leaning toward Carol):
Now, please, for one hour I've been trying to come to the point of—

Carol pushes him back as she apparently sights friend across room, calls, and waves, disregarding J. Lawrence.

CAROL (enthusiastically):
Hello, Georgie!

Displeased, J. Lawrence follows her glance.

106.   INT. SPEAKEASY   FULL SHOT
Carol and J. Lawrence in foreground, as Carol waves and calls to good-looking young man seated at small table with male companion. Young man smiles politely and waves back.

CAROL (calling):
Why weren't you there after the show last night? (Turning back at once to J. Lawrence.) Such a nice boy, Georgie—of such *good* family— (She looks down at bracelet on wrist.)

107.   CLOSE SHOT   CAROL AND J. LAWRENCE
Carol fingers bracelet, with reminiscent smile.

CAROL (wistfully, continuing):
—and *so* generous!

J. Lawrence frowns. As if reminded of man by bracelet, she turns again and waves off with melting smile. J. Lawrence's frown deepens.[16]

108.   MED. SHOT   MAN AND MALE COMPANION
at other table as man waves back to Carol.

FRIEND:
What's this Georgie business?

125

MAN (puzzled):
It's a new one on me.

FRIEND:
Who is she?

MAN (shaking head):
Never saw her before in my life!

Both men stare across toward Carol.

109. FULL SHOT FOUR AT TABLE
Carol turns back to J. Lawrence.

CAROL:
I'm sorry. You were saying—? (Before J. Lawrence
can speak.) Oh, give me my compact. I must look
simply frightful. (Again quickly changing subject as
waiter hovers near.) May we have some more champagne?

J. Lawrence, bewildered, tries to do everything at once—
give her compact, order, etc. Carol busies herself using
lipstick.

Trixie's hand is on Peabody's knee as she drinks, looking soulfully into his eyes. Smiling fatuously, feeling effect of champagne, Peabody lets his hand fall on hers as
if unaware of what he does. Trixie calls attention to it with
reproving shake of head.

TRIXIE:
Uh-unh!

PEABODY (removing hand):
I beg your pardon.

TRIXIE:
No . . . no . . . it's all right, Fanny.

Trixie replaces his hand on hers. Peabody sees J. Lawrence regarding him and withdraws hand quickly.

PEABODY (a bit thickly):
 I want a cigarette.

He pulls out cigarette and lighter. Trixie takes it from him, squealing in delight.

TRIXIE:
 Oh, let me see. Oh—platinum! (Reaches for his cigarette.) Let Trixie light it for you.

PEABODY (fussed):
 No, I can light it myself—

TRIXIE (reproachfully):
 Ooooooh!

Peabody surrenders cigarette. Trixie puts cigarette in her mouth, lights it, and hands it back to Peabody, who blinks tipsily, then tries to hide his pleasure by regarding lipstick-stained cigarette with assumed disapproval. Ostentatiously drops cigarette in ashtray and lights another for himself.

TRIXIE (again reproachful):
 Ooooh!

Meanwhile, another round of champagne has appeared on table. Carol's whole interest seems centered now on her drink.

J. LAWRENCE (a troubled look at his watch):
 I'm a busy man, Miss Parker, and I cannot afford to waste more time in coming to an understanding with you—

Carol leans toward him as he speaks, staring intently into his eyes.

CAROL (as if she had not heard him):
 I've been wanting to ask you a question. (J. Lawrence regards her, seriously.) Are your eyes hazel?

J. LAWRENCE (bewildered):
My eyes?

CAROL (nods):
Uh-huh!

J. LAWRENCE (provoked):
Miss Parker, please—

CAROL:
They *are* hazel. Nice eyes—they have such a kind expression.

J. LAWRENCE (not daring to like it as he'd like to, coughs nervously):
Miss Parker—

CAROL (pouting prettily):
Don't be so formal. You promised to call me—Polly!

At this moment Fay flutters up to table, obviously eager to meet the two men. Peabody and J. Lawrence rise politely.

FAY (effusively):
Hello everybody!

CAROL (coolly):
Hello.

TRIXIE (groaning):
Just when I was beginning to feel happy!

Carol and Trixie devote themselves to their wine, leaving Fay standing. She gives Peabody a melting look. Peabody and J. Lawrence wait awkwardly, expecting introductions.

FAY (to girls):
Introduce me, won't you?

TRIXIE (sarcastic):
Oh, I thought you'd gone. This is Fay Fortune, Mr. Bradford.

J. LAWRENCE (bowing with dignity):
How do you do.

FAY (putting it on strong):
Charmed.

Peabody reacts to Fay's flirtatious glances. Trixie sees the byplay, makes no move to introduce him to Fay.

PEABODY:
You haven't introduced me.

TRIXIE (annoyed):
Oh! Miss Fortune—Mr. Peabody.

FAY (gushing):
Mr. Peabody!

PEABODY (fatuously, glowing at her interest):
Miss Fortune! (Then with heavy-footed humor.) My *good* fortune.

TRIXIE (kidding him):
My good man, are you by any chance punning?

PEABODY (a giggle):
Oh, I'm quite a punster.

TRIXIE (sarcastic):
I get it. You probably were stroke on your college punsing team.

PEABODY (tittering):
Oh, dear, that's funny. That's very funny. (To Fay.) Won't you join us, Miss Fortune?

FAY (eagerly):
Love to! I'm just in the mood.

She sits quickly beside Peabody, who helps her to champagne. Trixie regards them with mounting anger.

PEABODY (very attentive):
Champagne?

FAY:
> Oh, indeed. My doctor recommends it.

Fay gives him the works with her eyes and he loves it.

PEABODY (sentimentally):
> Did you have a mother—?

FAY:
> What?

PEABODY:
> Whose name was Eunice?

FAY (thinking hard):
> No, I think not . . . (She thinks again.) I did have a mother—named Gertrude.

PEABODY (regretfully):
> You look like Eunice.

Fay gives him a languishing look. Trixie is burning up.

TRIXIE (sweetly to Fay):
> Darling, you *do* look like Eunice.

Trixie, as she smiles at Fay, kicks her savagely in the shin, unseen by Peabody.

FAY:
> Ouch!

PEABODY (solicitously):
> What is it?

TRIXIE (quickly):
> Fay has an attack of chiseling. It's chronic.

Trixie leans close to whisper in Fay's ear.

TRIXIE (savagely, whispering to Fay):
> One more look at him with those boudoir eyes and I'll break your leg! (Turning sweetly to others.) Excuse me for whispering. Fay and me have *so* much in common.

WIPE OFF TO:

110.   INT. HOTEL SUITE
Peabody, coat and collar off, vest unbuttoned, with a bad hangover, sits in armchair, wetting towel in basin on table beside him. J. Lawrence, in shirtsleeves, stands drying hands at bathroom door.[17]

J. LAWRENCE (severely):
Wasted the whole afternoon.

Peabody wrings out towel, begins wrapping cracked ice in it.

PEABODY (shaking head):
I warned you—I tried to tell you. If you'd listen to me . . .

Peabody leans back, putting improvised ice pack on aching head, with ludicrous effect as he closes eyes.

PEABODY (continuing):
She was a woman of the theater. Eunice was her name—Fuffy, she called me. Fuffy . . .

J. LAWRENCE (paying no attention to Peabody):
In a way it isn't wasted, completely. (Peabody nods with reminiscent sigh.) It's given me an idea. (Peabody's eyes open.) This girl is not stupid. She's smart. The way she maneuvered the thing so we couldn't come to the point—no senator could do more with a filibuster.

He chuckles appreciatively as he tosses towel off into bathroom. Peabody during J. Lawrence's speech has surreptitiously taken lipstick-stained cigarette from vest pocket—souvenir of the gay afternoon—and looked at it with relish, unseen by J. Lawrence. Peabody, remembering, chuckles, too. J. Lawrence steps toward Peabody.

J. LAWRENCE (with disapproval):
I don't see anything funny.

PEABODY (replacing cigarette hastily in pocket):
I don't either. That experience I started to tell you about—when I was a gay young blade—

J. LAWRENCE (disregards Peabody's words):
We just can't accomplish our purpose in a minute. It's going to take time. Now, I tell you, there's only one thing to do. One thing. (Begins to pace, thinking hard.) I don't want to do it, but I don't see any other way. We've got to spend more time here—we've got to see more of her—

PEABODY:
I don't wish to see any more of her. What I've seen convinces me—

J. LAWRENCE (ignoring him):
We must go to the limit, we must spend money, we must drink champagne, buy expensive trinkets—we must, we absolutely must make that girl think we're an easy proposition, suckers, you might say. (Peabody shakes head.) What are you shaking your head for?

PEABODY:
I'm just thinking of the consequences.

J. LAWRENCE:
So am I. I'm thinking of my brother and my responsibility to him. I believe I can make this girl transfer her affections from him to me—

PEABODY (as if he hadn't heard right):
What?

J. LAWRENCE (hastily):
Don't misunderstand me. Nothing personal in it. This girl is smart. This girl is after the money. I'll convince her that I'm the one that has most of the family wealth—and *then* I show her up for the

scheming little person she is. And *then* Bob comes to his senses!

He sits down, satisfied. Peabody shakes his head, worried.

J. LAWRENCE:
>*Now* what are you shaking your head for? Are you afraid?

Peabody clears his throat uncertainly, wanting to see more of the alluring Trixie, but fearful of his own susceptibility. He heaves up out of his chair indignantly.

PEABODY (bluffing):
>Afraid? Of what?

J. LAWRENCE (reflectively):
>I confess I'm a little afraid. That girl is very fascinating. But we're not boys, are we?

PEABODY:
>Hardly.

J. LAWRENCE:
>We're men, and we needn't succumb to that sort of feminine allure, need we?

PEABODY:
>No, we needn't.

J. LAWRENCE:
>Just because they want something we don't have to give in, do we?

PEABODY:
>No, not at all.

J. Lawrence picks up cigarette, holds out hand to Peabody.

J. LAWRENCE:
>Let me have a light.

Peabody flushes—stammers—then crosses to table, gets match, holds flame for J. Lawrence.

J. LAWRENCE (eyeing him severely):
Where's your lighter?

PEABODY (embarrassed):
My lighter—oh—uh—that's—uh—

WIPE OFF TO:

111. INT. GIRLS' NEW APARTMENT
CLOSE-UP PEABODY'S LIGHTER

CAROL'S VOICE OFF:
Where'd you get the lighter?

TRUCK BACK TO:

112. CLOSE SHOT TRIXIE AND CAROL
Trixie, sitting, has lighted cigarette and gazes comfortably at lighter. Carol stands by her.

TRIXIE (with satisfaction):
Fanny gave it to me.

113. INT. LIVING ROOM NEW APARTMENT FULL SHOT
Polly looks on curiously from couch where she sits with Brad.

BRAD (surprised and delighted):
Fanny! Say, this is wonderful! This is *marvelous!*

POLLY:
Who's "Fanny"?

TRIXIE:
Fanny is Faneuil H. Peabody, the kind of man I have been looking for. Lots of money and no resistance.

BRAD (laughing):
Old Peabody is the family lawyer . . . Oh, gosh, this is rich!

POLLY:

I don't think it's so funny— We must tell Brad's brother the *truth*.

TRIXIE:

Truth about what?

POLLY:

About Carol not being Polly.

BRAD (serious):

No . . . You've got to go on with it. He thinks it's pretty darn smart. Take him for a ride.

Trixie rises, showing presents she and Carol have already got from Peabody and J. Lawrence.

TRIXIE (gleefully):

You said it! Let's go on playing this game. It's for prizes. Look what I got already.

She takes cigarette case from her bag, holds it up in one hand.

TRIXIE:

Gold! (Holds up lighter in other hand.) Platinum! And that's nothing to what I'm going to get out of Fanny.

POLLY (shaking head):

I don't think it's right. It will only cause Brad more trouble.

CAROL (with indignation):

I wouldn't go on, except for one reason. Your big brother's idea of the theater and the people in it is what burns me up. We're all gold diggers and all parasites. I'd like to show him. I'd like to teach him a lesson, he'd *never* forget!

TRIXIE:

That's right, honey. Go into your dance.

CAROL (enthused):

Listen, I can do something that will make him come to Polly on his knees and beg her to marry Brad. I've got an idea!

Polly and Brad rise and crowd around Carol.

CAROL (continuing):

He thinks I'm Polly, doesn't he? All right, I'll *be* Polly. Polly, the chiseler. I'm going to make him gimme, gimme, gimme till he'll be so disgusted he'll be willing for Brad to marry anybody just so long as it isn't me.

BRAD (nodding):

That's not a bad idea. Of course, we're going to a lot of unnecessary trouble. I'd marry Polly with or without his consent—

Trixie is aghast at idea of losing this opportunity.

TRIXIE:

What do you mean—unnecessary trouble? How much is your income from the estate?

BRAD:

Forty thousand a year, more or less.

TRIXIE:

Unnecessary trouble! Say, I'll do all your worrying for you and a little hand laundry on the side for half of that.

CAROL:

You might as well have it, Brad. Polly *and* the money. Why not?

TRIXIE (strongly):

Besides, we want our fun. We got to have laughs.

CAROL (emphatically):

And I want to get even with him!

TRIXIE (blissfully):
And I want a chauffeur with a car. A chauffeur with
buttons—and a uniform. And a poodle dog. I want
a poodle dog—named Fanny!

Trixie and Carol are visualizing results of the conspiracy.
Brad and Polly look at them doubtfully, then exchange
trusting smiles.

DISSOLVE TO:

114. INT. PET SHOP   CLOSE-UP   POODLE DOG
that looks like Peabody, as Trixie holds it.

TRIXIE'S VOICE OFF:
Buy the little doggie for Trixie.

PAN UP TO:

115. CLOSE-UP   PEABODY
regarding dog (plant resemblance).

PEABODY:
What do you want the beast for?

TRIXIE'S VOICE OFF:
To have something to remember you by.

Peabody's face registers surprise and some annoyance.

116. FULL SHOT   PEABODY, TRIXIE, AND SALESMAN
as Trixie holds poodle up beside Peabody. Salesman tries
to hide amusement.

SALESMAN:
What name do you wish engraved on the collar?

TRIXIE:
Fanny.

SALESMAN:
It's—uh—not that kind of a dog, Madam.

TRIXIE (indicating Peabody):
His name is Fanny. Pet name.

SALESMAN:
Oh!

TRIXIE (turning to Peabody, sweetly):
Every time I look at my dog I'll think of you. (Peabody smiles weakly.) Hold him for me.

She hands dog to Peabody and begins to powder her nose. Peabody looks at dog, then off at mirror holding dog up beside face.

INSERT   MIRROR
reflecting Peabody's and poodle dog's faces, side by side. The dog yawns widely. Peabody's jaw drops. Peabody sees ludicrous resemblance; his face registers mixed emotions. He is not sure whether or not to be offended.

FADE OUT

FADE IN
INSERT   CLOSE-UP   THEATRICAL MAGAZINE
Illustration of new Roof Garden Night Club, with caption announcing gala opening, with members of Barney's company as guests of honor. Caption over still:
GALA OPENING FOR NEW ROOF GARDEN

Caption under still:

"Barney Hopkins and His Broadway Babies to Initiate New Night Spot as Guests of Honor."

TRUCK UP TO:

CLOSE-UP   ILLUSTRATION

Filling screen—no caption visible.

DISSOLVE TO:

117.   INT. ROOF GARDEN NIGHTCLUB   FULL SHOT   NIGHT
Duplicate of illustration, only now filled with movement. Festive air, tables crowded around dance floor, streamers, noisemakers, etc. Balconies with potted palms, divans,

tables, etc., visible in background overlooking lights of
city. Orchestra playing for "I've Got to Sing a Torch Song"
number, led by Fay, in black.

TRUCK UP TO:

118.   FULL SHOT   DANCE FLOOR NUMBER
Fay singing two choruses of "I've Got to Sing a Torch
Song" at white piano.

"I've Got to Sing a Torch Song"
(Chorus)
I've got to sing a torch song
For that's the way I feel
When I feel a thing, then I can sing,
It must be real
I couldn't sing a gay song
It wouldn't be sincere
I could never croon a happy tune
Without a tear
I have my dreams but one by one
They vanish in the sky,
I try to smile and face the sun
But romance passes by, that's why
I've got to sing a torch song
To someone far apart
For the torch I bear is burning there
Right in my heart.

[© 1933 WARNER BROS. INC. Copyright Renewed. All Rights Reserved.
Used by Permission.]

119.   FULL SHOT   CIRCULAR TABLE AND PARTY
All our principals about table, dance floor in background.
J. Lawrence between Carol and Polly. Brad on Carol's
other side pretending jealousy of her marked attention to
J. Lawrence. Peabody, next to Polly and Trixie beside
him.
    Peabody is showing great interest in Fay's number, as
she sings verse under scene. This irks Trixie. Carol is

139

trying to stimulate J. Lawrence's disapproval by behaving outrageously, calling for drinks, etc., but pouring most of her drinks on floor. J. Lawrence does not seem to mind, is drinking plenty himself, as Carol keeps filling up his glass. As Fay's number ends Peabody applauds vociferously.

TRIXIE (coldly):
You think she's good, don't you?

PEABODY (beaming):
Marvelous. She reminds me so of Eunice. Have I ever told you—

TRIXIE (interrupting, annoyed):
You have.

Trixie sharpens knife elaborately on tablecloth.

PEABODY (to Trixie):
What are you doing, Trixie?

TRIXIE (with meaning):
Sharpening a knife.

Carol is waving and shouting greetings to persons at other tables. Music starts; people rise from tables and begin dancing. J. Lawrence leans toward Carol.

J. LAWRENCE:
Shall we dance?

CAROL (putting on a tipsy manner):
Sure—certainly—why not?

J. Lawrence gets up. Carol rises a bit unsteadily. Brad rises, too, pretending to be jealous.

BRAD (jealously):
May I have this dance?

J. LAWRENCE:
Sorry, Bob. (Indicating Polly.) Why don't you dance with this nice young lady?

BRAD (sitting down grumpily):
Thanks . . . I'll dance with whom I choose.

J. Lawrence and Carol dance off.

PEABODY (to Trixie, indicating dance floor):
Shall we indulge?

TRIXIE (rising):
Okay. What can I lose!

She pulls Peabody out of his chair, and they bounce off
on dance floor.

120.   PAN SHOT   CAROL AND J. LAWRENCE DANCING

J. LAWRENCE:
My brother's jealous.

CAROL:
He has no reason to be.

J. LAWRENCE:
I'm not prepared to say that.

CAROL:
Then I'll say it for you.

J. LAWRENCE:
I'm much more the sort of man for you, Polly.

CAROL:
Yes. You have your good points.

121.   MED. SHOT   BRAD AND POLLY AT TABLE

BRAD:
Let's dance.

POLLY:
Don't look at me that way. He may see you.

BRAD:
Am I registering jealousy, or am I not?

POLLY:
>Oh, you're wonderful! (Looking off.) Watch it . . .
>look jealous. Here they come.

Brad and Polly rise and dance away together.

122.   CLOSE PAN SHOT   CAROL AND J. LAWRENCE DANCING
Carol is dancing very close to him, arm close about his
neck.

CAROL (snuggling even closer):
>You think it's vulgar, don't you, dancing this way?

J. LAWRENCE:
>I think it's delightful.

Carol promptly pulls away from him so there is daylight
between them. J. Lawrence looks disappointed.

123.   FULL SHOT   TABLE
Peabody and Trixie dance into scene. They sit at table.

PEABODY (apologetically):
>I'm a clumsy sort.

TRIXIE:
>You're a dear.

PEABODY (dropping into his chair):
>I'm getting old.

TRIXIE:
>Who isn't? I'm beginning to age a bit myself.

PEABODY:
>You! Old! Why you're the very personification of
>youth.

Gratified, Trixie makes motions of a curtsy.

TRIXIE (really pleased):
>Thanks. But honest, I don't know what's the matter
>with me lately. I have a yen for a little house in the

country with a fireside and carpet slippers for the old
man.

PEABODY:
And *who* is the old man?

TRIXIE:
You'd run if I tell you.

PEABODY:
Oh, I couldn't run very far or very fast.

TRIXIE:
Something's gone haywire. I'm getting sentimental.
Me, the most hard-boiled dame on the dirty white
way—

PEABODY:
You're not hard-boiled. That's just on the surface.
Underneath you're—

TRIXIE:
Say, what do you know about me underneath?

PEABODY:
I mean—

TRIXIE:
I know what you mean, you old sugar. Better watch
out or I'll fall in love with you. And boy, when love
comes at our age—

Trixie breaks off, pats Peabody's hand. Fay, having
changed costume for evening gown, enters behind Peabody, puts hands over his eyes. Trixie looks on disgusted.

FAY:
Guess who?

PEABODY (brilliantly):
It's little Fay!

FAY (as if amazed and pleased):
Ye-e-e-es!

TRIXIE (rising):
Oh, Fay, darling—

FAY (annoyed):
What?

TRIXIE:
Fay, darling, I want to show you something.

With assumed cordiality Trixie takes Fay's arm and leads her away from table. Trixie points off.

TRIXIE (her voice hard):
See what?

FAY:
What?

TRIXIE:
Can you read? Where it says Exit.

FAY:
Exit?

TRIXIE (nods venomously):
Start walking and keep walking and if you ever come near him again, I'll break *both* your legs!

FAY (drawing herself up):
I could easily resent that.

TRIXIE (pinches Fay's behind; Fay's "ouch" is topped with music):
Now scram!

Fay goes. Trixie returns to table.

PEABODY:
Did little Fay cry out?

TRIXIE:
No, it must have been the cornet you heard.

CUT TO:

124.   MED. SHOT   NEAR TABLE

at which two men and two girls are seated. Gigolo Eddie, wearing a tuxedo and carrying an open hat, meets Fay as Fay leaves Trixie.

CUT TO:

125.   CLOSE SHOT   OF THE TWO

GIGOLO EDDIE (in low voice):
How you coming?

FAY (with an angry backward glance in Trixie's direction):
I could build up a nice little business, but Trixie won't let me get near the old guy.

GIGOLO EDDIE:
That's all right. I got a nice delivery here. See you later.

CUT TO:

126.   MED. CLOSE SHOT

Fay moves on. Gigolo Eddie sits down at the table with the two men and the two girls. He takes out four pint bottles from hat, which he hands to the men and which they put under the table. Gigolo Eddie then clicks the hat shut. The man signs for the bottles on the label of the hat.

MAN (to Gigolo Eddie):
Have one with us?

GIGOLO EDDIE:
Sure. I'm not afraid of my own stuff.[18]

127.   FULL SHOT   DANCE FLOOR

Brad and Polly pause in foreground as music ends. There is spatter of applause as couples wait for encore. Polly nudges Brad and points toward Carol and J. Lawrence in background. Brad nods and starts toward them as Polly moves away toward balcony. CAMERA TRUCKS with Brad to:

128.   MED. SHOT   CAROL AND J. LAWRENCE
on dance floor. As music recommences, J. Lawrence starts
to take Carol in arms again. Brad taps him on shoulder.

BRAD:
   This is mine.

CAROL (to J. Lawrence):
   I'm sorry.

J. LAWRENCE (stiffly):
   Quite all right.

Carol snuggles into Brad's arms as they start to dance. J.
Lawrence watches displeased, then turns away, sees Polly
off, and starts toward balcony to join her.
   As they dance, Carol and Brad watch J. Lawrence go.
Carol whispers to Brad, he nods, they stop dancing and
leave dance floor.

129.   FULL SHOT   TRIXIE AND PEABODY .
at table in foreground, J. Lawrence crossing to balcony in
background as dancing continues. Brad speaks to Gigolo
Eddie at table, who grins and rises, while Carol signals to
Trixie. Trixie excuses herself to Peabody, rises, and joins
Carol. Carol, Trixie, Brad, and Gigolo Eddie slip unobtru-
sively toward balcony.

130.   FULL SHOT   BALCONY
Polly stands looking out at night sky and lights of city.
Dance music off. Couples dancing in background. J.
Lawrence comes out and joins Polly.

J. LAWRENCE (after a moment):
   Beautiful, isn't it?

POLLY (softly, very naive):
   Beautiful!

He watches her appreciatively. Unseen by them Carol,
Trixie, Brad, and Gigolo Eddie stealthily come out on bal-

cony and stand out of sight behind some palms, watching.

J. LAWRENCE:
> I've been watching you and wondering. You're so obviously a girl of breeding— (Polly regards him big-eyed.) Who were your people?

POLLY (wistfully):
> My father— (Hesitates.)

131. REVERSE ANGLE
Trixie and Carol listening in foreground with Brad and Gigolo Eddie; in background beyond palms, Polly and J. Lawrence.

POLLY (continuing):
> My father was an official in the government service.

TRIXIE (nudging Carol):
> Her father was a letter carrier!

132. CLOSE SHOT   POLLY AND J. LAWRENCE
He nods understandingly.

POLLY (emotionally):
> Mother—was an invalid.

133. CLOSE SHOT   TRIXIE AND CAROL

TRIXIE (grinning):
> Her mother could have licked John L. Sullivan.

Carol gestures her to be quiet.

134. FULL SHOT   POLLY AND J. LAWRENCE
as he pats her hand sympathetically, the other four visible in background watching.

J. LAWRENCE:
> Then how did a girl like you—? What are you doing in the theater?

POLLY (after a moment's pause):
Well, you see it's like this . . . I was at finishing school—when my parents died and I was left—(Her voice quavers, breaks.)

J. LAWRENCE (gently):
An orphan.

Carol and Trixie exchange delighted grins. Then the four put heads together as Carol gives Gigolo Eddie instructions.

POLLY (acting):
Yes. An orphan. So—I had to find something to do— earn money—and all I could find was—(A helpless gesture.) You see—

J. LAWRENCE (moved, tenderly):
I *do* see.

Gigolo Eddie now comes from behind palms as if slightly tipsy, pauses by J. Lawrence and Polly, stares at her, then grins familiarly.

GIGOLO EDDIE (to Polly):
Hey—Say, I know you—

Polly recognizes Gigolo Eddie, pretends surprise and to be insulted. J. Lawrence frowns.

GIGOLO EDDIE (continuing):
You're what's her name—Yeah, you're the little stuck-up dame goes home right after the show. (His voice is loud.) Listen, I've asked you a dozen times to step out with me and I'll spend money on you, kid. (Leering.) I'll spend money like a bootlegger. (Polly turns away distastefully.) Now don't go on saying no to me—

J. LAWRENCE (interrupting):
If she says no, that's her business.

GIGOLO EDDIE (sneering):
Oh, so *you're* trying to muscle in on her.

J. LAWRENCE (angrily):
Move on. You're drunk.

GIGOLO EDDIE (shakes finger wisely at J. Lawrence):
I'm not so drunk I don't know what's going on. (Winks broadly.)

J. LAWRENCE:
I said move on.

GIGOLO EDDIE:
I'm telling you, pal, you're wasting your time. We're all wasting our time. Can't get to first base with her. (Chuckles nastily.) She *ain't* the type.

J. Lawrence takes angry step toward Gigolo Eddie, who shrugs with careless wave of hand and starts away.

GIGOLO EDDIE (positively):
You're just wasting your time.

Gigolo Eddie goes.[19] J. Lawrence turns back solicitously to Polly, whose attempts to hide her amusement appear like near-weeping. Carol, Trixie, and Brad in background have enjoyed the scene.

J. LAWRENCE:
A shame you should be subjected to things like this.

POLLY (like a martyr):
Oh, I don't really mind.

Carol and Brad and Trixie start over casually, overhearing J. Lawrence's words.

J. LAWRENCE (very sincerely):
You're the sort of child who—sort of girl who—not cheap—not vulgar—not at all like people of the theater— (Suddenly.) You know—*you're* the girl my brother should be interested in!

Carol nudges Brad and bursts in angrily, walking on scene.

CAROL (to J. Lawrence, loudly):
I don't like that!

BRAD (taking cue from Carol):
Neither do I!

CAROL (sarcastically):
So we're all too vulgar for Mr. J. Lawrence Bradford.

J. LAWRENCE (seriously):
No, not at all.

CAROL (indicating Polly):
Except this little girl. I'm too cheap—too—vulgar!

J. LAWRENCE:
I don't mean that at all.

Carol tosses her head, turns angrily away, and hurries toward table. J. Lawrence follows her, trying to explain. Trixie, Polly, and Brad exchange grins of understanding and trail after them.

135. FULL SHOT PARTY'S TABLE
as Carol enters, apparently furious, grabs up wrap from her chair and gloves from table. J. Lawrence is at her shoulder remonstrating. Peabody at table regards them in stupid surprise.

J. LAWRENCE (to Carol):
You misundertsood! I think you're—

CAROL (interrupting):
I'm going home. I don't have to stay here and be insulted!

She starts away unsteadily in pretended fury. J. Lawrence hurries after her as Brad, Polly, and Trixie come in to table. Peabody rises uncertainly.

PEABODY (to Trixie, uncomfortably):
Let's go.

TRIXIE:
No.

PEABODY (pleading):
Yes.

TRIXIE (sitting down):
No.

PEABODY (weakly):
Yes!

TRIXIE (definitely):
No!

PEABODY (sadly):
No!

Peabody drops into chair again as Trixie reaches for drink.
WIPE OFF TO:

136. INT. LIVING ROOM   GIRLS' NEW APARTMENT   NIGHT
as Carol enters, still in assumed anger, followed by J.
Lawrence still trying to explain. She snaps on lights,
tosses evening wrap on chair. J. Lawrence, a bit awkwardly, grasps her hands.

J. LAWRENCE (pleading):
You must let me make you understand—I wouldn't
offend you for the world!

CAROL (pulling away):
Oh, let's forget about it.

She crosses to radio bar, getting out bottles and glasses,
soda and ice.

CAROL (still acting):
Have another drink!

J. Lawrence shrugs, face serious, and tosses down his

overcoat as Carol mixes drinks. He stands watching her, perplexed, visibly moved by her alluring charms. Carol comes back to him, holds out glass, with forgiving, seductive smile.

CAROL:
    I'll forgive you. Bottoms up.

J. Lawrence gulps down his drink nervously. Carol regards him over rim of glass as she sips. J. Lawrence starts to put glass down but Carol captures it and pours him second stiff drink, hands him glass.

J. LAWRENCE (glass in hand, stammering):
    I want to say—I—about you—I—

CAROL (coquettishly, as he hesitates):
    Like me?

J. LAWRENCE:
    Like isn't the word.

Carol trills a pleased laugh, turns away, and lights two cigarettes. J. Lawrence drains his second drink, puts down glass, and steps closer to Carol, his speech a bit thick.

J. LAWRENCE:
    It goes deeper than that, Polly.

Carol steps close to J. Lawrence and places lit cigarette between his lips. Her own lips smile invitingly. J. Lawrence quickly removes cigarette, tossing it aside in ashtray and again seizing Carol's hand.

J. LAWRENCE (strongly):
    I don't understand it myself—but—I love you, Polly.

Carol tries unsuccessfully to free her hand.

CAROL (queer tone):
    You're drunk.

J. LAWRENCE (fiercely):
    No, I'm not—I'm—

He sweeps her into his arms. She struggles, pushing un-availingly against his chest.

CAROL:
> Yes. You are—you're drunk.

J. Lawrence silences her with a passionate kiss; he is al-most as surprised as she. She draws back in his embrace, looking at him in disconcerted alarm.

J. LAWRENCE (in a rush):
> I love you, Polly.

He kisses her again—a long kiss. She lets him, likes it in spite of herself, returns it, her arm tightening about him. Then, in sudden revulsion of feeling, Carol draws back, again trying to push him away, her eyes wide, startled, almost frightened.

CAROL (breathless):
> You don't mean a word you're saying . . . You're playing, aren't you . . . ? I am, you know . . .

For answer, J. Lawrence holds her tighter than ever, tries to kiss her again.

CAROL (struggling):
> Now stop, I—

His lips on hers stiffle her speech. She lends herself to it, relaxing, snuggling close in his arms. Suddenly his arms loosen; she pulls back to look at him, misty eyed. Without warning, J. Lawrence's eyes go glassy; he staggers, his arms dropping by his side, stumbles, and falls across chaise longue, dead drunk. Carol stares at him, sur-prised, indignant, hurt, disappointed.

CAROL (almost a sob):
> You *are* drunk.

As Carol looks down at J. Lawrence, out cold, and won-dering what to do next, there comes a loud startling knock at the door. Carol gasps, stares at door apprehensively.

CAROL (her voice shaky):
Who's that?

TRIXIE'S VOICE OFF:
It's me! Trixie.

Relieved, Carol hurries to open door. She is trembling, close to hysterics.

CAROL (as Trixie enters):
Where's your key?

TRIXIE (holding up key):
Here it is. But I can't manage it. My fingers are frost-bitten.

CAROL:
What happened to Fanny?

TRIXIE:
I left Fanny behind. He's waiting.

As she crosses into room, Trixie sees J. Lawrence breathing stentoriously, sprawled on chaise longue, his eyes closed. She stops short, staring in great amazement.

TRIXIE (raised eyebrows):
What's the matter with him? Sleeping sickness?

CAROL (pitifully, tears starting):
He's passed out.

TRIXIE (eyeing him indignantly):
Well, he don't have to pass out all over my chaise longue. (Gasping with a sudden inspiration.) Saaaay!

CAROL:
Say what?

TRIXIE (in delight):
Have I an idea? Ask me: Have I an idea?

CAROL (smiling wanly):
Have you an idea?

TRIXIE (catching Carol excitedly by shoulders):
Listen. We stick him in bed, your bed.

CAROL (stiffening, angrily):
Oh no, you don't!

TRIXIE:
Don't get excited. You sleep with me.

CAROL (momentarily mystified):
Oh.

Trixie almost dances with joy over her grand idea as it develops.

TRIXIE (gleefully):
When he wakes up, will we have him where we want him? Will he do just exactly what we want him to do? Ask me, will he?

CAROL (shakes her head):
I don't like it.

TRIXIE:
You want to get even with him, don't you?

CAROL (bitterly):
Yes, I do.

TRIXIE:
Well—can't you see him—can't you see him waking up in the morning in bed—your bed? What will he ask himself—what would anyone ask himself? "What has happened?" he will ask himself. "What am I doing in this girl's bed?" And how many answers are there to that? How many? You tell me.

CAROL:
Oh, but—nothing *will* have happened.

TRIXIE:
No, of course not. Nothing *will* have happened.

CAROL:
You said it!

TRIXIE:
But *he'll* think— Say, all those big stuck-up ideas he
has about himself—He'll have lost every one of them.
He'll feel like a—what do they call those guys—oh,
yes—a *cad!* (Holds up hands showing midget size.)

Carol looks down at J. Lawrence in bitter scorn, then
turns to Trixie in sudden decision, nods agreement.

CAROL:
It's a bet! I'll do it!

TRIXIE (happily, with gesture):
Take his head.

CAROL (pushing Trixie toward his head):
I'll take his feet. You take his head. I don't want to
have to look at him.

TRIXIE (a queer look at Carol):
You know, I thought you were kind of getting stuck
on him—

CAROL (a harsh laugh):
Don't be stupid, Trixie. I've just been putting on a
good act.

They start to lift J. Lawrence.

TRIXIE:
A very good act. You fooled me.

DISSOLVE TO:

137.   INT. BEDROOM   NEW APARTMENT
J. Lawrence on bed, still out cold. Carol stares at him with
mixed emotions, Trixie moves about room decorating it
with intimate bits of lingerie as well as J. Lawrence's coat,
tie, etc., to give the effect of having been carelessly scattered about.

TRIXIE (as she works):
> And I guess you think I'm falling for that apple-cheeked boyfriend I've been chiseling. Say, you'd be surprised what plans I've got for him. And will *he* be surprised. I'm going to take him like Grant took Waterloo, or whatever he took. (Tucks J. Lawrence in.) There now, my little man.

Trixie surveys with satisfaction the general dissipated effect she has created. At this moment Polly and Brad appear in the door.

TRIXIE (to Carol):
> Now when he wakes up in the morning—

Brad enters, picks up her words, singing them. He is followed by Polly.

BRAD (singing):
> When he wakes up in the morning—

Brad sees J. Lawrence on bed and breaks off in amazement.

BRAD:
> Say, what's this—? Oh no. It can't be! It isn't! (He grins.)

TRIXIE:
> It is!

BRAD:
> How did *he get there*?

TRIXIE:
> He passed out. So we tucked him in.

BRAD (delighted):
> Oh no. This is marvelous. It's a panic.

POLLY (worried):
> I'm afraid we've gone too far.

BRAD:
Gone too far! *No.* It's only the beginning!

He laughs so hard he has to drop into chair.

TRIXIE (suddenly remembering):
Say, I have to run. I have something important to attend to. (As she hurries out.) I'll be back . . . in an hour or so.

Brad rises and stands over unconscious J. Lawrence. Polly and Carol watch with mixed emotions.

BRAD (orating):
My dear brother, so you'll stop my income, will you! Won't let me marry Polly, will you? Listen, old fellow— You don't know it yet, but you're going to wake up a kinder and wiser man . . .

He breaks off in a laugh.

FADE OUT

FADE IN

138.   INT. FURNISHED APARTMENT   PARLOR   NIGHT
Cozily arranged small room is softly lit, suggestive of secluded "love nest." This is to be identified later as Gigolo Eddie's apartment. Peabody's hat and coat are on chair. Peabody, tie askew, dress shirt rumpled, waits impatiently. He is a bit drunk and uncertain of himself. He lights cigarette, paces a couple of unsteady steps, lays cigarette down on ashtray, to pull out and inspect watch. Returns watch to pocket, shaking head, then lights another cigarette. Paces again. Notices, passing mirror, condition of tie, puts down second cigarette, tries to straighten tie, manages to get it untied, and gives up. He sighs and lights third cigarette. Again paces. Suddenly finds other two lit cigarettes smoking and is puzzled. A bit befuddled, looks around to see if any other persons are present. Shakes head vaguely and puts out all the cigarettes. Door opens and Trixie enters.

PEABODY:

 I was beginning to think you were playing a joke on me. You gave me a key to this place and told me to make myself at home, and then I thought you weren't going to show up.

TRIXIE (greeting him affectionately):
 Well—here I am, honey. Here I am. Calm yourself.

She tosses off her wrap.

PEABODY (embarrassed):
 You know—what you said to me tonight—?

TRIXIE (with glance at clock):
 Now what was it I said—

PEABODY:

 About the little house in the country and the old man— (Growing sentimental.) Oh, my dear, you remind me so of—

TRIXIE (interrupting):
 Eunice.

PEABODY:

 No. Not Eunice. You remind me—I don't know how to say this—it seems absurd at my age—but every man has a woman of his dreams— (Trixie regards him strangely) who'll be his friend, his sweetheart, companion of his joys and sorrows—in brief, to wit, his wife. My dear—

Peabody has taken Trixie's hands during his impassioned declaration and drawn her close to him. At this moment the door bursts open. Peabody starts back surprised as Gigolo Eddie enters, brandishing revolver and scowling.

GIGOLO EDDIE (fiercely):
 I thought something like this was going on!

Pretending panic, Trixie screams, clinging to Peabody.

PEABODY (alarmed):
Who is this man?

TRIXIE (a moan):
My husband!

PEABODY (to Trixie; eyes popping in alarm):
Why didn't you tell me you were married?

GIGOLO EDDIE (threateningly):
Don't put on that innocent stuff. You knew it.

PEABODY (to Trixie):
I didn't know it. I never broke up a home in my life.

TRIXIE:
Oh, this is terrible. I don't know what to say.

PEABODY:
How could you do a thing like this?

GIGOLO EDDIE (quickly):
We hadn't been living together. Just the same, I'm
her husband. (Grimly.) And now, if I was you, I'd
take out my checkbook—

PEABODY:
Money?

GIGOLO EDDIE (sarcastic):
You're a mind reader.

PEABODY (turns to Trixie; bitterly):
It was unfair of you not to tell me. I loved you, Trixie.
I was going to ask you to be my wife.

Trixie has watched the scene with increasing discomfort
as conscience pricks her. Now Peabody's sincerity and
real hurt move her to action. She drops her pose of "discovered wife" and becomes herself. She looks at Peabody
ruefully, then turns to Gigolo Eddie, jerking her head toward door. Peabody regards her with amazement.

TRIXIE (brusquely):
Scram, Eddie. It's all off!

GIGOLO EDDIE (surprised):
What?

TRIXIE (wearily, to Eddie, nodding):
I'm reneging. (Turns to Peabody.) He's not my husband. He's a phony. (Peabody stares.) Honey, I can't go through with it. You thought I was a cheap chiseler, so I was going to be a chiseler—but the trouble is, Fanny—

She breaks off, can't go on, chokes a bit.

PEABODY:
What is the trouble?

TRIXIE (blubbering):
I love you, Fanny.

Peabody beams happily, puts arms around Trixie.

PEABODY:
There, there, child. I love you, too. That's what I've been trying to tell you—I want to be your little Fanny for life—

Gigolo Eddie watches, surprised.

GIGOLO EDDIE (shaking his head):
I can't figure dames out. (Resignedly.) Well, I guess this is one on the house. (Goes to a connecting door and opens it, calls.) Fay! Oh, Fay!

FAY'S VOICE OFF:
Coming.

GIGOLO EDDIE:
Bring in the business, will you?

Fay wheels in a baby buggy, as Peabody looks up in surprise. Gigolo Eddie pulls back the curtain from the baby buggy, takes out a couple of bottles.

GIGOLO EDDIE (to Fay, indicating Trixie and Peabody):
    The deal's off. They're going to get hitched.

TRIXIE (handing Eddie a bill):
    Here's the ten bucks for the use of your apartment.

FAY (to Trixie, indicating Peabody):
    You mean you're *really* in love with him?

TRIXIE:
    I'm afraid I am.

FAY (walking over and putting her arm around Trixie in a friendly way):
    If I'd known you were really serious, I'd never have tried to cut in on you the way I did.

TRIXIE:
    I guess I had you wrong, Fay. You must have a heart hidden away somewhere after all.

FAY:
    There are a lot of things you don't know about me. (Indicating Gigolo Eddie.) For instance, Eddie and I have been married for over a year.

TRIXIE:
    Oh, so it's legal!

GIGOLO EDDIE:
    Let's everybody have a drink.

PEABODY (rubbing his hands together in pleased manner):
    Splendid. Splendid.

All four sit down cozily, as Eddie pours the drinks.[20]

FADE OUT

FADE IN

139.   INT. BEDROOM   GIRLS' NEW APARTMENT   NEXT MORNING
        CLOSE-UP   J. LAWRENCE
on rumpled bed, just coming out of it. He opens eyes,

blinks at strange room, sits up bewildered. He looks around in growing horror.

140.   PAN SHOT   AROUND ROOM   FROM J. LAWRENCE'S ANGLE
It is obviously a woman's bedroom. Dress, stockings, pretties as well as his own things are strewn about. J. Lawrence groans off scene.

141.   FULL SHOT   J. LAWRENCE ON BED
He sits, trying to remember what happened after that kiss. His head aches abominably, his mind is a blank—anything may have happened. Suddenly he listens aghast. A feminine voice, off, begins to carol gaily. J. Lawrence winces, climbs gingerly out of bed. There comes sound of a shower, off, and feminine gurgles at cold spray.

142.   FULL SHOT   BEDROOM
Dismayed, J. Lawrence starts toward door in B.V.D.'s, wanting to peek and see who is singing, but hesitates, afraid, and starts to dress. Gets trousers, shoes, and shirt on, picks up coat, collar, and tie, and starts to sneak out on tiptoe. He is just reaching door when it bursts open and Brad stalks in, apparently furious. He looks at J. Lawrence with supreme contempt. J. Lawrence can only stare miserably back, speechless.

BRAD (in righteous indignation):
    And you were the one who called other people cheap and vulgar. Well, I'm listening. Make it good.

J. LAWRENCE (gulps):
    What am I doing here?

BRAD:
    I'll bite. What *are* you doing here?

J. LAWRENCE:
    I haven't the least idea how this happened.

BRAD:
>   You probably walk in your sleep. You don't know in whose bed you are, do you?

J. LAWRENCE:
>   No. It seems to be a—a—woman's.

BRAD:
>   Bright boy! It is a woman's.

J. Lawrence looks around again, then sits on bed in utter despair, dropping coat, collar, and tie.

BRAD (putting on his act):
>   My brother—the brother I admired and respected—the head of the family—the trustee of the estate—not only does it, but lies about it.

J. LAWRENCE (miserably):
>   I don't remember doing anything and I'm not lying about it.

BRAD:
>   The girl I love—the girl I want to marry.

Brad's suffering is superb. J. Lawrence holds up pajama top that is lying on bed.

J. LAWRENCE:
>   Is this—?

BRAD (as if broken-hearted; bitterly):
>   Yes, it's hers.

J. LAWRENCE (groans):
>   Oh! Oh, I begin to—I have a hazy recollection the last thing I— I give you my word I didn't realize— I don't know what to say— I—

BRAD:
>   Don't say anything. I'm grateful to you. Grateful. You've opened my eyes. I'd never marry her now.

J. LAWRENCE:
No, of course you—after this—

BRAD:
Sure, you don't care who I marry, anyone but the girl
I love. Well, I don't care either now. Just to show
her—I'll marry anyone. I'll marry the first girl I see—
no matter who she is.

There comes a meek little knock at door. Both men turn
as door opens. Polly enters carrying tray.

POLLY (sweetly):
Good morning.

J. LAWRENCE (suddenly to Brad):
You know what you just said. The first girl—

BRAD:
Yes, I know what I said—

POLLY:
I brought you some orange juice and black coffee—

Polly crosses and puts tray down by J. Lawrence, with
not so much as a look at Brad.

J. LAWRENCE (taking her hand, gratefully):
My dear child—

BRAD (harshly, to Polly):
Never mind that "dear child" bunk. Stay away from
him. He's utterly untrustworthy—a hypocrite! Will
you marry me?

Polly acts startled, looks at J. Lawrence, who nods, vio-
lently, yes. Polly turns to Brad, her eyes sparkling, but
hiding her delight.

POLLY (to Brad):
Yes.

Brad grasps Polly's hand, turns sharply to J. Lawrence.

165

BRAD:
Is that okay with you?

J. LAWRENCE:
Certainly. It's very okay with me.

BRAD (to Polly):
Come on.

Brad clasps Polly in his arms for a big kiss, then drags her out the door backwards. J. Lawrence stares after them.

143.   INT. HALL   OUTSIDE BEDROOM DOOR
as Brad and Polly enter from bedroom, closing door after them. Joyously Brad clasps her in his arms. They kiss, then Polly pulls loose, smiling but worried.

POLLY:
Now what will happen?

BRAD (happily):
Now, lady, you and I will get ourselves married.

POLLY (anxiously):
But what'll he do—when he finds out?

BRAD (confidently):
Nothing much. In six months I'll be twenty-one.

POLLY (dubiously):
In six months.

BRAD (putting arm around her):
Let's not worry about it. Let's get married. Then we can worry.

They start out.[21]

144.   INT. BEDROOM   NEW APARTMENT
J. Lawrence still sits on bed staring at closed door, confused, with mixed emotions. He shakes head, sighs deeply, picks up coat, collar, and tie, and with a last rueful look at his "bed of shame" starts cautiously out of room.

145.   INT. LIVING ROOM   NEW APARTMENT   DAY
J. Lawrence tiptoes in, crosses to pick up hat and coat from chair where he left them the night before. He pauses, looks down remorsefully at Carol's evening wrap; his hand touches it gently. Trixie's voice startles him.

TRIXIE (grimly):
    Good morning.

J. Lawrence turns to find Trixie regarding him from dinette door.

J. LAWRENCE (abject):
    Good morning.

He turns and starts for door.

TRIXIE (tauntingly):
    How would you like your eggs?

J. Lawrence just shakes his head and continues to door. His hand is on knob when Trixie's voice arrests him.

TRIXIE (brutally hard):
    Say, where do you think you're going? Do you think you're going to do what you did and just get away with it? Ruin a girl's future and all just because she loves you?

J. Lawrence stares at her dully, his head aching.

J. LAWRENCE:
    I don't know where I am or what you're saying.

TRIXIE (advancing belligerently):
    Well, that's just too bad. I'll tell you where you are—

J. LAWRENCE:
    Oh, I know where I am all right. I mean figuratively speaking, I'm confused. I don't know what's happened.

TRIXIE:
    Well, I do. Plenty, brother—*plenty!*

J. LAWRENCE:
Then tell me. What do you want me to do?

TRIXIE (indicating chair by desk):
Sit down. (He sits meekly.) How much is it worth to you?

J. LAWRENCE:
Worth? For what?

TRIXIE:
Oh, call it payment for a night's lodging, if you like.

J. LAWRENCE:
You don't mean this. Polly doesn't know—

TRIXIE:
Say, listen, what do you think Polly is?

J. LAWRENCE:
I never would have believed it! And yet, why not? What else have I the right to expect?

TRIXIE:
You said it, what else?

J. LAWRENCE (pulling out checkbook):
Here. Let's be quits.

J. Lawrence starts to write check. Trixie hides her triumphant smile.

J. LAWRENCE (as he writes):
Five thousand. Is that satisfactory?

TRIXIE:
It is not. What do you think we are, anyway? This isn't the Mills Hotel.

With a bitter shrug, J. Lawrence tears up first check and makes out another. He rises and hands it to Trixie stiffly.

J. LAWRENCE:
Here. Ten.

Trixie regards check with evident satisfaction. J. Lawrence gathers coat, etc., and moves toward door.

J. LAWRENCE (severely):
    And this is all I'll do.

TRIXIE:
    Oh, don't feel generous about it. It's not much.

J. LAWRENCE (pausing):
    That's your opinion. Now, have you any objections
    if I go on my way?

TRIXIE:
    Objections? Let me open the door for you.

Trixie steps to door and with exaggerated politeness holds
it wide.

J. LAWRENCE (stiffly):
    Thank you.

TRIXIE (coldly):
    Not at all. Come back when you can't stay so long.

J. Lawrence goes. Trixie closes door after him, then,
chuckling, hurries into bedroom.

146.   INT. SECOND BEDROOM   GIRLS' NEW APARTMENT
        MED. SHOT   CAROL AT DRESSING TABLE
        sitting, head in her outstretched arms, crying her heart
        out. Reflected in mirror we see door open and Trixie gal-
        lops in joyfully, waving check.

TRIXIE'S VOICE OFF:
    I got it.

Carol gulps, blows nose tearfully, without looking around
at Trixie.

CAROL:
    Got what?

Trixie enters scene, shoves check under Carol's nose.

TRIXIE (triumphantly):
Rest your eyes on this.

Carol pushes it away with renewed sobs.

TRIXIE (aghast):
What's the matter? Not enough?

CAROL:
I don't want it. I don't want any of it.

TRIXIE (reproachfully):
What's the matter with you? (Accusingly.) I knew it!
You *are* carrying the torch for that Back Bay codfish!

Carol turns slowly to Trixie, her eyes overflowing with tears.

CAROL:
I am not. I *hate* him!

TRIXIE (wisely):
Sure, you do. Why shouldn't you? He's got no more
feelings than a hyena.

CAROL (defensively):
He has too. Don't you talk that way about him.

TRIXIE:
Besides, we played him for a sucker. He's just a
chump.

CAROL:
He's not a chump. He's honest. He's good.

TRIXIE (wisely, nodding her head):
Sure. You hate him all right.

CAROL (sobbing miserably):
I love him . . . I've never been so happy in all my
life!

FADE OUT

FADE IN

147. CLOSE-UP   NEWSPAPER STORY
with pictures of Brad and the real Polly. Front page headlines read:

SCION OF SOCIETY MARRIES
MUSICAL COMEDY BEAUTY

At city hall today Robert Treat Bradford
of Boston and Polly Parker, this season's
musical comedy sensation, were married
by Judge etc., etc.

TRUCK BACK TO:

148. INT. HOTEL CORRIDOR   CLOSE SHOT   LOWER PART OF
DOOR
as bellboy's hand shoves paper in under door.

149. INT. J. LAWRENCE'S HOTEL ROOM
J. Lawrence in bathrobe and slippers lies on bed, feeling
miserable, eyes closed, wet towel lumped on his forehead. Peabody, somewhat abashed, walks nervously up
and down making his halting confession.

PEABODY:
I have a confession to make . . .

J. LAWRENCE:
Well . . . ?

Peabody pauses, embarrassed. J. Lawrence groans. Peabody looks, sees paper under door, picks it up without
glancing at it, and continues walking and talking, holding newspaper in his hand.

PEABODY (continuing, awkwardly):
Last night, I told Miss Lorraine—Trixie—that I care
for her deeply. (J. Lawrence sits up, surprised.) And
she admitted an equal affection for me.

J. Lawrence shakes his head sadly. Peabody continues,
gesticulating with paper.

171

PEABODY (sentimentally):
   For the first time in my life, true love, real love, with
   a real woman—

Peabody stops aghast as his eyes suddenly see the pictures. He clutches paper and reads headlines excitedly. J.
Lawrence regards him, puzzled. Peabody gulps, strides
over, and shoves paper under J. Lawrence's nose.

PEABODY:
   Look! Read that!

J. Lawrence takes one look, lowers paper, frowning at
Peabody, realizing he's been made a fool of.

J. LAWRENCE (slowly):
   I've been tricked.

PEABODY (nods agreement):
   You certainly have been.

J. LAWRENCE (taps paper angrily):
   This is the girl—she's the one Robert planned to
   marry all along—the one I intended to save him from.

PEABODY:
   No doubt about it. They've made a fool of you.

J. LAWRENCE:
   What about *you?*

PEABODY:
   Well! Now—I—

J. LAWRENCE:
   Did you know? If you knew why didn't you tell me?
   What did I bring you along for, anyway? To heave
   ridiculous, ponderous sighs at that giraffe—

PEABODY:
   Who are you calling a giraffe, sir? I have a suspicion
   it is the woman I love—

J. LAWRENCE:
You love! You give me a pain!

J. Lawrence swings feet to floor and rises, facing Peabody.

J. LAWRENCE:
You're coming along with me. I'll show them I'm not such an easy mark.

PEABODY (startled):
Where to?

J. LAWRENCE:
To that woman's house—the one who posed as Polly Parker—who led me on—

PEABODY:
I'll not go with you. I can't!

J. LAWRENCE:
Why?

PEABODY (uncomfortably):
I have an—engagement for dinner . . . a conference.

J. LAWRENCE:
Then I'll go myself. I'll show her—

J. Lawrence starts to remove robe, with quick angry decisiveness.

DISSOLVE TO:

150. INT. GIRLS' NEW APARTMENT   LIVING ROOM   EARLY
EVENING
J. Lawrence, glowering, faces a poised and smiling Carol.

CAROL (her voice hard):
But I never said your brother wanted to marry *me*, and I never *said* I was Polly!

J. LAWRENCE:
I took that for granted.

CAROL (almost a sneer):
You took too darn much for granted.

J. LAWRENCE:
I'll ask you to return my check, please.

CAROL:
Your check? (Laughs.) Oh—that's on exhibition. I knew you'd probably stop payment on it, anyway. (Indicates check, framed, hanging on wall.)

INSERT   J. LAWRENCE'S CHECK FOR $10,000
framed and hanging on the wall.

BACK TO SCENE:

J. LAWRENCE (beside himself):
I'll—I'll—take the necessary steps to—

CAROL:
You'll what? You've made a sap out of yourself and done your best to make a fool out of me. I don't want to ever see you again, understand? As for your check—you don't think I hold myself as cheaply as that, do you?

J. LAWRENCE:
Cheaply! Ten thousand dollars.

CAROL:
Well, that's your estimate of me. It's not mine. The check is framed—not cashed. I hung it up there to remind me never to get mixed up with your type again. And now, get out, will you. Please, get out.

J. LAWRENCE:
Oh, no, I won't get out.

CAROL:
Oh, yes, you will.

J. LAWRENCE:
Oh, no, I won't. First I'll tell you what I think of you.

J. Lawrence steps close to her. She puts fingers in her ears, nods toward door.

CAROL:
Get out.

J. Lawrence grabs her by the shoulders to shake her. Both are furious. Carol tries to tear herself loose.

CAROL:
Don't you dare!

They are very close. Suddenly J. Lawrence takes her in his arms, she resists.

J. LAWRENCE (fervently):
I was drunk last time—but I'm *not* drunk now—and I mean it. I love you—Polly—

CAROL (weakly):
I'm not Polly.

J. LAWRENCE:
Whatever your name is.

CAROL (her voice breaking):
Carol— That's my name— Cheap and vulgar Carol— daughter of a Brooklyn saloon keeper and a woman who took in washing— That's me— Carol—torch singer in Coney Island joints—cheap and vulgar— (He kisses her.)

J. LAWRENCE (smiles at her adoringly):
Every time you say cheap and vulgar, I'm going to kiss you.

CAROL (quickly):
Cheap and vulgar—cheap and vulgar—cheap—

J. Lawrence silences her with three quick kisses. They smile happily at each other. Carol relaxes, resting her head comfortably on his shoulder.

CAROL (sighing ruefully, but happy):
> I didn't want to fall in love with you. I was only play-
> ing a game.

J. LAWRENCE (grinning):
> I didn't want to fall in love with you, either. I was
> trying to play a little game myself.

CAROL:
> But, darling—you do forgive Brad and Polly?

J. LAWRENCE (grim again):
> I do not.

Carol pulls back in his arms, looking at him.

CAROL (reproachfully):
> Oh, you *must*.

J. LAWRENCE:
> If they're married—

CAROL (quickly):
> They are. They phoned from city hall . . .

J. LAWRENCE (decisively):
> I'm going to have their marriage annulled.

CAROL:
> But you said yourself—

J. LAWRENCE (interrupting):
> I don't care what I said. I was upset—confused.

CAROL (struggling to free herself):
> Maybe you're confused now—about us—

J. LAWRENCE (not letting her go):
> No. That's one thing I'm *sure* about. But their mar-
> riage is off—definitely off!

CAROL (firmly):
> Then *so is ours!*

J. LAWRENCE:
    You mean you won't marry me?

CAROL:
    I certainly do!

J. Lawrence tries to hug her. She jerks away, notices clock, suddenly frantic.

CAROL:
    Gee gosh! The show—I'm late.

Carol grabs up hat and coat, making for the door.

CAROL (as she goes):
    Sorry—see you later.

J. LAWRENCE (following her):
    But, Carol—you haven't told me— We've got to settle this—

The door bangs shut after Carol. J. Lawrence frowns thoughtfully, looks at framed check on wall, studies it a moment gravely, then with sudden grim decision takes it down and stuffs it, frame and all, in his pocket.

DISSOLVE TO:

151.   INT. THEATER   FULL SHOT   STAGE
        Show is in progress—production number—with Carol on stage in costume. Music of orchestra off.[22]

152.   BACKSTAGE CORRIDOR
        Stage manager knocking at dressing room door, music continues off.

STAGE MANAGER (calling sharply):
    On stage!

He moves away down corridor as door opens and Polly and Brad in costume come out blissfully hand in hand and start toward stage, CAMERA TRUCKING with them. As they reach door of next dressing room it, too, opens and Trixie, in costume, and Peabody, likewise hand in hand,

come out. The two couples meet and hurry along corridor, CAMERA TRUCKING with them, music growing louder.

PEABODY (grinning proudly):
    Congratulate us. We're man and wife.

BRAD (surprised):
    You're not.

TRIXIE (applying extra rouge):
    I'm the bride. I ought to know—

POLLY (hugging Trixie):
    Oh, Trixie, I'm *so* glad.

BRAD (beaming):
    We're married, too.

PEABODY (shaking hands, as they walk):
    My heartiest congratulations.

BRAD:
    Same to you.

POLLY:
    Isn't it wonderful?

PEABODY (smiles):
    At my age?

TRIXIE:
    At *any* age.

They reach stage. Stage manager hurries them toward
wings.

STAGE MANAGER:
    Come on. Step on it.

153.   MED. SHOT   IN WINGS   BACKSTAGE THEATER
The four (Trixie, Polly, Brad, and Peabody) run into Carol
making her exit from stage after her number, burst of applause off. Chorus scurries about in background as or-

chestra starts playing Brad and Polly's next number. Trixie grabs Carol's hands.

TRIXIE:
> I got him—signed, sealed, and delivered.

CAROL:
> Good girl. Keep him close to home.

TRIXIE:
> You bet. Right on a leash.

BRAD:
> Have you seen my esteemed brother since he heard the news?

CAROL:
> Yes. And whatever happens—don't weaken.

The stage manager bustles up. Chorus in background on stage is doing number, leading up to Brad and Polly's entrance.

STAGE MANAGER:
> Come on. Come on. Your cue.

Polly suddenly sees J. Lawrence storming toward them from stage door entrance, a man who looks like a detective with him. Polly grasps Brad's hand, scared. Brad faces him bravely. Stage manager tugs at Brad's arm impatiently.

J. LAWRENCE (scowling):
> Wait a minute. I hear you two are married. (Brad and Polly nod.) I'm going to have it annulled.

PEABODY (putting arm around Trixie):
> You can't annul our marriage.

J. LAWRENCE:
> Not yours, stupid! *His.* (Indicating Brad.)

BRAD:
> You can't do that.

J. LAWRENCE:
Yes, I can. You're under age!

154.   FLASH   OF COMPANY ON STAGE
stalling and waiting for Brad and Polly.

155.   MED SHOT   GROUP IN WINGS

STAGE MANAGER (frantic, tugging at Brad and Polly):
Get out there! Get out there!

POLLY:
You wouldn't do it.

CAROL:
You mustn't. *Please!*

BRAD:
You've interfered enough. We're married and we're
going to stay married.

156.   FLASH   OF BARNEY   ON OPPOSITE OF STAGE
gesturing frantically to Brad and Polly to go on.

157.   MED SHOT   GROUP IN WINGS
Brad stands his ground as stage manager pushes him. J.
Lawrence pauses dramatically, frowning. Carol puts her
hand pleadingly on his arm.

CAROL (to J. Lawrence):
Listen, today you asked me to marry you—

BRAD (amazed):
He did!

J. LAWRENCE:
Yes. I proposed to her and I was sincere.

CAROL (furiously):
If you do this to Polly and Brad I'll never marry you
in a million years. I told you that once and I meant
it.

J. LAWRENCE (stiffly):
As much as I love you, nevertheless, I'm determined to look after my brother's interests whether he likes it or not. (To detective, indicating Brad.) Arrest him. You have the warrant . . . Perjury—falsification of age in obtaining a marriage license.

BRAD:
You can't hold me on that.

DETECTIVE:
Technically we can—pending an investigation. (He takes Brad by the arm.)

POLLY:
Oh, Brad, what will we do?

158.   FLASH   OF ORCHESTRA LEADER
bewildered. He signals orchestra to keep on vamping for entrance of Brad and Polly.

159.   MED. SHOT   GROUP IN WINGS
Barney rushes in, very excited.

BARNEY (fuming):
What's going on here? What's holding up the show? (To Polly and Brad.) Why don't you get out there and do your number? Do you want to ruin me?

BRAD (bitterly):
My brother's had me arrested—for getting married.

BARNEY (sputtering):
Arrested? Where's the cop?

J. Lawrence indicates detective, who pulls his hat down over his eyes and half turns away.

J. LAWRENCE:
Here is—Detective Jones.

BARNEY (impatiently, after a quick glance):
Detective, my eye. I know that mug. He's a *ham actor!*

DETECTIVE (drawing himself up):
That's no way to speak of an artist. I've played with
Sir Henry Irving, George Arliss, David Warfield—

BARNEY (interrupting):
Scram! You've been a washout all up and down
Broadway for twenty years! (To Polly and Brad.) Well,
what are you waiting for? Get on out there! Go into
your number! Has everybody gone bugs?

Polly and Brad heave a sigh of relief and start out on the
stage.

J. LAWRENCE (stopping them):
Wait a minute! (Pulls out framed check.) Here.

Brad takes framed check, mystified.

BRAD:
What's this?

J. LAWRENCE (with a sudden grin):
I'm sure Carol will endorse it to you—for a wedding
present!

BRAD (surprised):
Ten thousand dollars!

He looks at Carol, who nods emphatically.

BRAD:
What a brother!

J. LAWRENCE (arm around Carol):
You mean—what a *sister-in-law!*

As Polly, delighted, kisses Carol, Brad quickly turns to
fire alarm box, breaks glass of framed check, stuffs check
in pocket, returns frame to J. Lawrence, grabs Polly by
hand, and dashes out onto stage where they lead chorus
doing "Shadow Waltz."

160.   FULL SHOT   STAGE   PRODUCTION NUMBER
Brad and Polly leading "Shadow Waltz" number.

"Shadow Waltz"
(Chorus)
In the shadows let me
Come and sing to you
Let me dream a song that
I can bring to you
Take me in your arms and
Let me cling to you
Let me linger long
Let me live my song;
In the winter let me
Bring the spring to you
Let me feel that I
Mean ev'rything to you
Love's old song—will be new
In the shadows
When I come and sing to you, dear,
In the shadows
When I come and sing to you.

During number, CUT IN

161.   FLASH   PEABODY AND TRIXIE   IN WINGS
embracing and reacting to mood of song.

162.   FLASH   J. LAWRENCE AND CAROL   IN WINGS
in long, happy kiss.

163.   FULL SHOT   STAGE
"Shadow Waltz" merges into big production number of
"We're in the Money" with Brad and Carol leading it.

"We're in the Money"
(Chorus)
We're in the money
We're in the money
We've got a lot of what it takes
        to get along
We're in the money
The skies are sunny
Old man depression, you are thru,
        you done us wrong
We never see a headline
'Bout a bread-line today
And when we see the landlord
We can look that guy
Right in the eye
We're in the money
Come on my honey
Let's spend it—lend it—send it
Rolling around.

As curtain falls on grand finale,

FADE OUT

THE END

Notes to the Screenplay

1 Production details of the "We're in the Money" number (formally titled "The Gold Diggers' Song") offer insight into what the Busby Berkeley approach required to stage this kind of number. Fifty-four girls were used; their costumes were made up of fifty-four thousand "silver" coins; five silver dollars, twenty-eight feet in diameter, formed the background; and dozens of "gold" pieces ten feet wide served as props to be manipulated during the dance routines. (The coins were duplicated in chocolate and aluminum and used as promotional giveaways.)

Ginger Rogers, in singing the lyrics, breaks into a chorus using Pig Latin. The press book explains the genesis of this business: "She had hummed the tune so many times she sang the words in Pig Latin to vary the monotony. Director Mervyn LeRoy heard her, and was struck by the novelty of the queer play of words. He ordered Ginger to sing in Pig Latin when the shot was taken. So Ginger's own version is in the picture."

The lyrics of all the songs in this Revised Final script differ slightly from the lyrics heard in the film.

2 From the number of appearances he makes in the shooting script, it appears that Gigolo Eddie was to be used as a kind of Greek chorus or leitmotif. The idea was obviously abandoned. Eddie appears at the beginning, middle, and end of the film, but his role is inconsequential.

3 A considerable amount of dialogue in this scene—approximately the last three-fourths—is not in the film.

4 In the film, Aline MacMahon uses a pair of fireplace tongs to lift the milk bottle off a fire escape.

5 Scenes 37 through 44 do not appear in the film.

6 Before Fred Astaire teamed with Ginger Rogers in the thirties, he and his sister, Adele, comprised a famous Broadway dance team that was featured in many important productions in the twenties.

7 The newspaper clipping, or newspaper story, is used often in the film as a device for foreshortening the narrative.

8 The name of Barney's show is *Forgotten Melody*, billed as the "Greatest Review of All Time, with All-Star Cast."

9 Lumbago, a rheumatic inflammation of the lumbar region, used to be one of those sure-to-get-a-laugh diseases—like gout.

10 This number contains several elaborate choreographic effects—many things that obviously could not be performed on a theater stage. An overhead camera is used to provide some interesting, geometric effects. In order to stage the number, Berkeley had to build an entire park set on the sound stage. In this particular number—which follows life in the park through four seasons—he uses every opportunity to show off the pulchritude of his chorus girls. (See figure 10.)

11 The exchange in scenes 81–83 is a little hard to believe. Journalists, even critics, do not share scoops with one another.

12 This number was shifted to the end of the film where it serves as the finale. See pages 27–30 for a discussion of its content and intent. As a result, scenes 160–63 are not in the film.

13 A major portion of the dialogue in this scene is not in the film.

14 This excerpt from the 1974 *National Park Service Guide to the Historic Places of the American Revolution* explains the derivation of Peabody's given name: Boston's "Faneuil Hall, called the 'cradle of Liberty,' served as a market place, town hall, and meeting house during the Revolutionary movement. It now contains some very fine Revolutionary paintings, a library, and a military museum." Besides the obvious connection with the Back Bay Boston sophistication as represented by J. Lawrence and Peabody, the diminutive of the name ("Fanny") provides an opportunity to satirize Peabody, whom we see occasionally making an ass of himself.

15 The only apparent logic for the new apartment seems to be that now that the girls are back to work, they are able to afford more expensive digs. The apartment is decorated in a most attractive Art Deco motif, which adds to the period charm of the film.

16 Scenes 105, 106, and 107 are compressed in the film.

17 The material at the beginning of this scene is omitted in the film.

18 Scenes 118, 124, 125, and 126 are not in the film.

19 The Gigolo Eddie material in this scene is not in the film.

20 None of scene 138 is in the film.

21 Scenes 142 and 143 are not in the film.

22 The "Shadow Waltz" number was inserted here. It offers another example of Berkeley's complex and visually stunning choreography as well as some unique special effects, including chorines dancing on a gracefully curving ramp, playing neon-outlined violins (see figures 19 and 20), and wearing three-tiered hoop skirts made of two thousand yards of white China silk. The Warners press book points to the

elaborate preparation that preceded the shooting of the number: "Seventy-five women worked eight days to make these costumes and at the last minute, two milliners sat up all night to create fifty-four silver wigs of metallic cloth with little sequin tendrils in front giving the appearance of curls."

As if that wasn't enough, Mervyn LeRoy reveals, "The first day we rehearsed that number, the Los Angeles area was shaken by a moderate earthquake. The ramp swayed and several of the girls fell. Fortunately, none of them was seriously hurt. The ramp had to be repaired, however, before we could shoot the scene."

It was also reported that LeRoy smoked an average of twenty-five cigars a day (up from his usual dozen) while working on the film—a manifestation, no doubt, of his apprehension that another earthquake might swallow them all up before the project was complete.

Production Credits

Directed by	Mervyn LeRoy
Screenplay by	Erwin Gelsey and James Seymour
Dialogue by	David Boehm and Ben Markson
Based on a play by	Avery Hopwood
Music and lyrics by	Harry Warren and Al Dubin
Photography by	Sol Polito
Film Editor	George Amy
Art Director	Anton Grot
Gowns by	Orry-Kelly
Numbers created and staged by	Busby Berkeley
Vitaphone Orchestra conducted by	Leo F. Forbstein

Running time: 96 minutes
Released: June 1933

Cast

J. Lawrence Bradford	Warren William
Carol King	Joan Blondell
Trixie Lorraine	Aline MacMahon
Polly Parker	Ruby Keeler
Brad Roberts	
(Robert Treat Bradford)	Dick Powell
Faneuil H. Peabody	Guy Kibbee
Barney Hopkins	Ned Sparks
Fay Fortune	Ginger Rogers
Don Gordon	Clarence Nordstrom
Dance director	Robert Agnew
Gigolo Eddie	Tammany Young
Delivery boy	Sterling Holloway
Elderly gentleman	Ferdinand Gottschalk
Gold Digger girl	Lynn Browning
Sheriff	Charles C. Wilson
"Pettin' in the Park" baby	Billy Barty
Black couple	Snowflake (Fred Toones)
	Theresa Harris
Chorus girl	Joan Barclay
Stage manager	Wallace MacDonald
Society reporters	Wilbur Mack, Grace Hayle,
	Charles Lane
Dog salesman	Hobart Cavanaugh
Dance extra	Bill Elliott
Critic during intermission	Dennis O'Keefe
Callboy	Busby Berkeley
Detective Jones	Fred Kelsey
First Forgotten Man	Frank Mills

This comprehensive cast list was compiled from the press book and from Paul Michael and others, eds., *The American Movies Reference Book* (Englewood Cliffs, N.J.: Prentice-Hall, 1969), p. 347.

Inventory

The following materials from the Warner library of the Wisconsin Center for Film and Theater Research were used by Hove in preparing *Gold Diggers of 1933* for the Wisconsin/Warner Bros. Screenplay Series:

Play (typescript), "The Gold Diggers," by Avery Hopwood, no date, annotated, 144 pages.

Treatment, "High Life," by Erwin Gelsey and James Seymour, November 29, 1932, 15 pages.

Treatment, "High Life," by Seymour, no date, 17 pages.

Treatment, "High Life," by Gelsey and Seymour, no date, annotated, 23 pages.

Treatment, "High Life," by David Boehm and Seymour, December 23, 1932, 26 pages.

Screenplay, "High Life," by Seymour, Boehm, and Ben Markson, February 3, 1933, 140 pages.

Revised Temporary, "High Life," by Seymour and Boehm, January 18, 1933, 107 pages.

Final, "High Life," by Seymour and Boehm, January 27, 1933, 145 pages.

Revised Final, "Gold Diggers of 1933," by Seymour, Boehm, and Markson, February 8, 1933, with changed pages to February 11, 1933, 146 pages.

DESIGNED BY GARY GORE
COMPOSED BY GRAPHIC COMPOSITION, INC.
ATHENS, GEORGIA
MANUFACTURED BY INTER-COLLEGIATE PRESS, INC.
SHAWNEE MISSION, KANSAS
TEXT AND DISPLAY LINES ARE SET IN PALATINO

Library of Congress Cataloging in Publication Data
Seymour, James.
Gold diggers of 1933.
(Wisconsin/Warner Bros. screenplay series)
"Gold diggers of 1933,
screenplay by James Seymour, David Boehm, and Ben Markson,
from the stage play by Avery Hopwood."
1. Gold diggers of 1933. [Motion picture]
I. Boehm, David, joint author. II. Markson, Ben, joint author.
III. Hove, Arthur. IV. Hopwood, Avery, 1884–1928.
Gold diggers of 1933. V. Title. VI. Series.
PN1997.G5684384   791.43'7   79–5402
ISBN 0–299–08080–3
ISBN 0–299–08084–6 pbk.

W W

The Wisconsin/Warner Bros. Screenplay Series, a product of the Warner Brothers Film Library, will enable film scholars, students, researchers, and aficionados to gain insights into individual American films in ways never before possible.

The Warner library was acquired in 1957 by the United Artists Corporation, which in turn donated it to the Wisconsin Center for Film and Theater Research in 1969. The massive library, housed in the State Historical Society of Wisconsin, contains eight hundred sound feature films, fifteen hundred short subjects, and nineteen thousand still negatives, as well as the legal files, press books, and screenplays of virtually every Warner film produced from 1930 until 1950. This rich treasure trove has made the University of Wisconsin one of the major centers for film research, attracting scholars from around the world. This series of published screenplays represents a creative use of the Warner library, both a boon to scholars and a tribute to United Artists.

Most published film scripts are literal transcriptions of finished films. The Wisconsin/Warner screenplays are primary source documents—the final shooting versions including revisions made during production. As such, they will explicate the art of screenwriting as film transcriptions cannot. They will help the user to understand the arts of directing and acting, as well as the other arts involved in the film-making process, in comparing these screenplays with the final films. (Films of the Warner library are available at modest rates from the United Artists nontheatrical rental library, United Artists/16 mm.)

From the eight hundred feature films in the library, the general editor and the editorial committee of the series have chosen those that have received critical recognition for their excellence of directing, screenwriting, and acting, films that are distinctive examples of their genre, those that have particular historical relevance, and some that are adaptations of well-known novels and plays. The researcher, instructor, or student can, in the judicious selection of individual volumes for close examination, gain a heightened appreciation and broad understanding of the American film and its historical role during this critical period.

WW

WISCONSIN/WARNER BROS SCREENPLAY SERIES

Titles in the Series

Now Available

The Adventures of Robin Hood
Gold Diggers of 1933
The Green Pastures
High Sierra
The Jazz Singer
Mystery of the Wax Museum
To Have and Have Not
The Treasure of the Sierra Madre

In Production

Air Force
42nd Street
Heroes for Sale
I Am a Fugitive from a Chain Gang
Little Caesar
Mildred Pierce
Mission to Moscow
The Public Enemy
The Roaring Twenties
White Heat
Yankee Doodle Dandy

Forthcoming

Arsenic and Old Lace
The Big Sleep
Black Fury
Black Legion
The Cabin in the Cotton
Captain Blood
The Corn Is Green
Dark Victory
Five Star Final
Footlight Parade
The Fountainhead
Key Largo
Marked Woman
A Midsummer Night's Dream
The Petrified Forest
Sergeant York
Taxi
Watch on the Rhine
Wild Boys of the Road

General Editor: Tino Balio

TINO BALIO is Professor in the Department of Communication Arts and Director of the Wisconsin Center for Film and Theater Research at the University of Wisconsin-Madison. He is the author of numerous articles in the field, the editor of *The American Film Industry* (Wisconsin, 1976), and the author of *United Artists: The Company Built by the Stars* (Wisconsin, 1975).

Editorial Committee: Dudley Andrew, John G. Cawelti, Dore Schary

DUDLEY ANDREW, head of the Film Division at the University of Iowa, is the author of *The Major Film Theories* (Oxford, 1976). JOHN G. CAWELTI, Professor of English and Humanities at the University of Chicago, is the author of several books, including *Apostles of the Self-Made Man* (Chicago, 1965), *The Six-Gun Mystique* (Bowling Green University, 1970), and *Adventure, Mystery, and Romance: Formula Stories as Art and Popular Culture* (Chicago, 1976). DORE SCHARY spent many years in Hollywood, where he wrote some forty screenplays before becoming a studio executive, vice president in charge of production at RKO, and eventually studio head of MGM. He is also an accomplished playwright (*Sunrise at Campobello*) and a popular lecturer on theater, film, and television subjects. He and Eleanore Griffin won an Academy Award in 1938 for their original story of *Boy's Town*.